Adios,
HAVANA

Andrew J. Rodriguez
A Memoir

D1397589

Outskirts Press, Inc.
Denver, Colorado

Adios, HAVANA
A Memoir
All Rights Reserved
Copyright © 2005 Andrew J. Rodriguez

Outskirts Press
http://www.outskirtspress.com

ISBN-10: 1-59800-048-9
ISBN-13: 978-1-59800-048-1

Library of Congress Control Number: 2005930713

Outskirts Press and the "OP" logo are trademarks belonging to
Outskirts Press, Inc.

Printed in the United States of America

CONTENTS

TO
Margarita

INTRODUCTION

"The only reason I'd ever buy a gun is to fight communism," my father said to me when I was eight years old, thirteen years prior to Castro's revolution and before I had enough sense to appreciate his distaste for words ending in "ism."

God only knows why Papa's remark became so deeply embedded in my mind. Was he some kind of wizard who could see thirteen years hence? Or was my guardian angel putting words in his mouth to ensure that I would always recognize the ominous implications of radicalism?

"It's a bad word, Andy, believe me! Communism is a very bad word," Papa said to me frequently.

How could it be worse than Cousin Pepito's swearing? I wondered. It couldn't be, I decided, or Mama would've shoved Palmolive soap into Papa's mouth.

Toward the end of World War II, Papa had bought a Philips short-wave radio to listen to the Voice of America. Virtually glued to his rocking chair, his right ear almost rubbing the cloth-covered speaker, Papa tried to catch bits of news from the front every single night. I would sit on his lap until ready to go to bed. Most people would rather listen to the soothing sounds of waves lapping onshore, or to the melodies of a Chopin nocturne, but not me. Even at sixty-five I still enjoy the evocative static of a short-wave radio at bedtime.

Who would have imagined then that during the late fifties, Papa would be upgrading to a Zenith Transoceanic to listen again to the Voice of America—the only transparent source of news from Cuba's Sierra Maestra Mountains where Fidel Castro and his guerrillas were drumming up their fateful revolution; the most purulent episode in the entire history of the alligator-shaped island?

Preceding the Fulgencio Batista coup of March 10, 1952, unseating president-elect Carlos Prio, and even during Batista's late term as president by thievery, hardships and contentment took their inevitable turns in Cuba, as they did elsewhere on earth. It wasn't until the last days of tyranny that desperation and greed turned this despot's repressive machinery against innocent civilians and the rebellious young. Formerly a sergeant- stenographer in the armed forces, Batista pulled his way up the ranks to become, on two different occasions, one of Cuba's most corrupt dictators.

Worshipped by the military, the *sargento*-turned-tyrant ruled the country for almost fifteen years, first as a result of the military rebellion of September 4, 1933, against Carlos Cespedes—interim president after the resignation of dictator Gerardo Machado—and then following his 1952 military coup against president-elect Prio.

Following this takeover, the self-appointed head of state ruled the country for seven consecutive years, until deposed by Castro...the next despot in line.

Have you ever wished you had the best of all possible worlds? Well, guess what? Cubans did at various times; but they didn't value it enough to protect it.

Do you want to know why their world fell apart?

I shall tell you, then. But first, let's be realistic: If you want to know the truth, my truth is that I may be risking book burnings and rotten mangoes hurled at me as I try to autograph and sell my memoirs. On the other hand, when an old geezer realizes that there isn't much time left to speak his mind, he needs to say whatever he wants, so I have decided to risk the fuss this introduction may bring to Miami's Little Havana, and express in the fewest possible words the main reasons these happy-go-lucky citizens lost their freedom and why in God's name their nation was and continues to be in such a mess.

So, my friend, pull up a chair, relax, have a martini, if that's what you drink; iced tea otherwise; and listen to my sizzling conclusions.

Once upon a time, oh Lord have mercy...in an island long ago identified by Columbus as *the most beautiful ever seen by human eyes,* lived a lucky group of people called Cubanos. Ironically, though, the captivating beauty and delightful climate of their land, the allure of its countryside, and their own naivety, seeded unto their society a careless joie de vivre and never-ending sense of humor that eventually weakened their concept of civic responsibility. In plain jargon: *Lo tiraban todo a relajo.* They took their problems in stride and everything else for granted.

A stranger might have considered these Cubanos, who argued constantly about politics and baseball, *peloteros* with a conscience; yet they didn't do much to extricate themselves from opportunists, demagogues, and chocolate soldiers. They talked, and talked loud, even waving their hands as they talked, but that was all. By allowing a carefree lifestyle to interfere with civic and patriotic obligations, they were endorsing corruption by neglect; always allowing the inevitable to occur before doing something about it...if at all.

As they lived the present and worshipped their past, these islanders seldom worried about the future. They realized freedom was costly, fragile, and volatile, but only a few understood the catastrophic effects of its abuse and neglect. They skipped and danced along a careless path toward a tropical nirvana, until they became suicidal by omission. Gold in their hands, seldom appreciated...thus it was lost. *Los Americanos siempre nos protegen.* The Americans always protect us.

But why were these Cubanos so naïve to think that America would look after them?

The answer: *El Tio Sam's* traditionally self-appointed right to intervene in any Latin American country that in his judgment undermined democracy, promoted hemispheric instability, or endangered US strategic and/or financial interests.

As long as Hopalong Cassidy and the Lone Ranger helped dictate US foreign policy, countless Cubanos felt confident that nothing could ever destroy their cheerful lifestyles. In an act of supremacy, rich and powerful Tio Sam kept his Latin neighbors under his thumb at all times.

But there was a catch in the northern giant's commitment to protect Central and South American stability—a wrinkle that contributed to the birth of "the ugly American" character and the "Yankee-go-home" attitude so prevalent in third world countries all over the world.

Besides Costa Rica—one of the few authentic democracies in the hemisphere—the majority of Latin American countries were ruled by cold-blooded gangsters and military dictators who were consistently blessed and supported by the rich uncle from the north. As a result, El Tio Sam's self-serving attitude was berated by most Latin Americans, especially the exploited poor. According to those with an inch of forehead and an ounce of pride, however, the powerful relative couldn't have cared less about democracy, as long as his interests, particularly those of the United Fruit Co. and other corporate protectorates remained untouched.

But the triumph of Castro's revolution against Batista in January 1959 changed Tio Sam's attitude toward Cuba. Upset at the new leader's audacity for nationalizing Standard Oil and other large American-owned corporations, the mighty Tio began to take reprisals against the Cuban government, creating a propitious situation for Fidel to cozy up to the Russians. And so the puzzling question of whether a communist government ninety miles from the rich uncle's backyard was a result of America's arrogance in matters of foreign policy, or Fidel's underhanded strategy to implement a communist paradise at any cost...or a combination of both, persists to this day.

"*Ese tio imperialista,*" Castro claimed in many of his speeches, "*is the common enemy of all people.*"

In short, the resentful and egocentric rabble-rouser happened to be in the right place at the right time and had the guts, the genius, and the drive to use with Machiavellian savoir-faire every opportunity to advance his deceptive political scheme. All else is hogwash.

Assets expropriated, with no strategic or financial resources to defend, and afraid of the Russians, Tio Sam stopped interfering in Cuban affairs, and the islanders were left adrift at the mercy of their new master: the Soviet Union.

American influence gone forever, the safety net existed no more.

These are damn good reasons why, after almost fifty years the Alligator Island still is in the same rotten mess. The Lone Ranger icon shattered, and a million Cubanos scattered all over the world.

Now that I've tried to answer the sticky question as quickly and politically correctly as I could, I shall launch this narrative by rewinding my imagination to Havana in the mid-fifties, and while at it, borrow from Dickens's masterpiece, *Tale of Two Cities,* the most fitting of all introductory lines:

"It was the best of times. It was the worst of times..."

And let it go at that.

I have learned from my ancestors that if every man writes a book, plants a tree, and fathers a child, the world around him will be more agreeable. This book is my tree. The roots reach back sixty years. Its fruits are still fresh.

Not a celebrity in any way, I'm a common man who feels compelled to share his memoirs with his adopted countrymen for the sake of reflection. Therefore, I shall raise my martini glass and propose a toast:

"May the story of our lives bring enlightenment to the blind, appreciation for our liberties in America, the resolve to learn from the past, and the tenacity to prevent negligence from tainting our country's self-determination... for centuries to come! Salud!

CHAPTER 1

In The Beginning,
There Was Cuba

That we may better understand some of the circumstances surrounding my story, I must be bold enough to say that cult and religion were two of the most important elements influencing our nation's character long before the revolution.

Let me tickle your imagination with an example to prove my claim.

Toward the end of the nineteen-fifties and right before the demise of Batista's dictatorship, a famous TV and radio personality declared himself a spiritual leader overnight, publicly claiming to possess supernatural powers to dissipate evil spirits, cure infirmities, assist in domestic issues, alleviate anxiety, cast out demons, and so forth.

In order to materialize his miracles, the self- appointed mystic instructed his countrywide audience to put a glass of water atop their radios and TVs day and night, especially while watching the program. The frenzy lasted several years, and by the thousands, people claimed to have witnessed miracles, healings, and apparitions. Almost the entire Cuban population had glasses of water scattered all over the house, and for those shy of admitting their "spiritual shortcomings," concealing them under the bed became the alternative of choice: Gullibility nonpareil.

From the times of slavery to the mid-nineteen-fifties, Afro-Cuban cults—passionate mixtures of Catholicism and Voodoo—made significant contributions, good and bad, to our value system, way of thinking, and artistic expressions so clearly evoked in Cuban music and literature.

Although I haven't determined when our nation became so mystified by cult and religion, I can offer you my own version on why it did.

Of the five million Cubanos living in the island during the nineteen-fifties, thirty percent were African-Cubans (blacks and mulattoes), ten percent

Asians and other extractions, and sixty percent Europeans, mostly of Spanish descent. Our country had no native Cubans, for they were enslaved and annihilated by the Spanish conquistadors.

Blacks and mulattoes were deeply attached to their African spiritual traditions, and those of Spanish descent to the lifestyles and religions of Western civilization, especially Catholicism.

In order for our egalitarian society to embrace the two main cultures, an accommodation ultimately ensued, so cults such as *santeria,* a combination of Catholicism and voodoo, emerged as a result.

While a great number of African-Cubans practiced santeria rituals, the majority of the population, including some blacks and mulattoes, followed the ways of Christianity.

The complexities that arose from merging African cults with Catholicism gave way to widespread superstition in a large segment of the population, especially the uneducated poor.

Here's another example.

Sometime in between dictatorships and the invention of the daiquiri, a legendary never-ending soap opera involving voodoo, slavery, and racism was tuned in every single night except on Sundays by most of the population. As a person walked the streets of Havana after dinner, one could follow the plot's development word by word and tear by tear just by strolling from house to house.

One of the story's main characters, a white landlord paralyzed from the nose down, was the only protagonist who knew the solution to a mystery. It took the disabled man weeks upon weeks of making guttural sounds to unravel syllable by syllable the mystifying solution to the riddle—the origin of his illegitimate mulatto son, Albertico.

After weeks of yarn-spinning, the contrite old man eventually healed by santeria, pronounced the revealing evidence and solved the protracted mystery. The novel's last broadcast and the Bay of Pigs invasion marked the only times I remember seeing the entire island come to a complete stop.

Nevertheless, I don't wish to convey the notion that because most Cubans were Catholics, religiousness ruled our way of life; no, not by a long shot, for the only times I saw churches filled to capacity were during *la Misa del Gallo,* or Christmas Eve Mass, and on Palm Sundays, when the faithful stood in endless lines for their free share of *guano bendito,* or blessed palms, later to be hung from bed boards, front doors, or rear view mirrors as insurance against bad times, disease, lightning, *mal de ojo* (evil eye), and so on.

One effect of growing up in a Catholic culture and being part of a large Catholic family was my mother's obsession with my taking the first communion before age fifteen. This caused a dramatic face-off that drove me nuts and her up a wall, for I adamantly refused to stand in line wearing a white suit, white patent leather shoes, and holding a candle, to take the first bite of the holy bread. Perhaps influenced by Papa's agnosticism, I had learned to loathe priests with a passion, and no one on earth was going to make me look that pure. The ritual was largely about righteousness, and I despised excessive goodness, for it was a sign of *sissiness* in Macho-land.

My mother's faith was so unyielding that in a last- ditch effort to convert me, she begged a Sunday school teacher from the local church to take me under her wing, "even against his will," she said, "because this boy needs someone to help straighten up his head."

Aware of her tremendous challenge, Ms.Suarez tried harder than any of her predecessors to teach me the catechism; but the kind lady became so badly demoralized by my antipathy to religion that she finally decided to send me home as irredeemable.

"Better abide by the holy sacraments or you'll be a heretic the rest of your life, young man." She waved an admonishing finger, but I couldn't see anything wrong with continuing to live in blasphemy.

Bent on obliterating my stubbornness, one day

Ms. Suarez invited me to her home for a scoop of homemade *mantecado*—vanilla ice cream—and to meet Cachita, a Brazilian parrot that knew more profanities than most of today's movie stars. The feathered creature belonged to a young nephew who had moved to a smaller apartment where wicked animals were not allowed.

Ms. Suarez, a spinster, was a generous and devoted woman, the kind who had much more in her head than religion alone; demons, damn it! Yes, she had more demons inside than the Devil himself. Demons forcing me to read over and over the boring holy book!

"I have one ticket left for the New Orleans Symphony Orchestra next Saturday at the Auditorium Theatre. Would you like to have it?" she asked casually. "It won't cost you anything, Andy, I promise. All you need to do is read the first ten pages of the catechism. Later on, if you want to attend another performance, I have more tickets, which means you'll have to study another ten pages. Now, what do you say to that, son?"

Not only were her tickets free, but they offered me a rare chance to catch the bus downtown without inventing excuses. *Hmmm*, I thought. *What a delightful opportunity!*

The performance at the Auditorium—Havana's venerated concert hall in the Vedado district—was so impressive that I kept exchanging tickets for pages. Not only did Ms. Suarez teach me some badly needed righteousness, but she also opened my ears to beautiful music. Yet, in spite of Mama's efforts, I never made it to first communion. The poor woman couldn't convince my doubting father...and that was too bad.

Inspired by a chapter of Cuban mythology proclaiming the divinity of doctors and by my godfather Julian, a small town obstetrician, I had always wanted to become a physician—not necessarily in his specialty, but a surgeon, sort of a demigod dressed in white. Definitely not communion white, but sterile white, with sterile gloves and sterile mask, like a bleached Spider Man fighting disease and removing ugly tonsils and appendices.

As a way of commitment to my ideal, I often practiced on chickens and the family dog, whom I saved from a generalized infection caused by bites suffered in a fight. Luckily, Cuban pharmacies dispensed drugs limitlessly and without prescriptions. After I applied sulfa and antibiotics orally and subcutaneously and stitched his many wounds, Crispin was good as new in less than two weeks.

Unbelievable as it may sound, one of my poultry-patients grew much larger than a rooster and laid goose-size eggs, thanks to a lengthy treatment with corticosteroids.

Every one in Cuba loved to play doctor, even if it was at the expense of his own life...or someone else's.

Available over the counter and in original containers, a person had to buy an entire bottle with a hundred pills, even if he or she needed only twenty. As a result, most homes had a *botiquin,* or drug arsenal, with enough ammo to annihilate every conceivable germ and treat every form of disease. Few ever ran out of tranquilizers, antibiotics, sulfa, pain Killers, sleeping pills and so on.

Every time a cold or flu threatened a party or a fishing trip, I stopped at the neighborhood drugstore for a shot of penicillin. The pharmacist charged me for the drug and I tipped him for the injection. The conundrum: drug addiction was virtually unknown among adolescents...I swear!

Unable to afford medical school, however, my parents encouraged me to take Public Accounting instead. What a bummer, for accountants didn't have a designated day to receive presents and laudatory calls, whereas doctors had December third reserved as *El dia del Medico.*

■ ■ ■

Professor Perez points at me. "Mr. Rodriguez, will you please stand up and explain to the class the importance of performing an acid test on a balance sheet?"

My gorgeous tan suddenly turns cadaveric. I have no idea what acid test the "Chimney Man" is talking about.

"I'm sorry, Professor, but I've never heard of such a thing." The class of fifty students roars with laughter.

A chain smoker, Prof. Perez taught cost accounting at the university at night and worked for one of Havana's most prestigious accounting firms during the day. Even though our conceited teacher constantly bragged about his fascinating career, I couldn't understand how anyone could fall so hard for such a boring profession. "It is the love of my life," he said repeatedly. *How can anyone say that*? I asked myself over and over. *Doesn't he crave excitement*?

In those days, university and high school students all over the country were known for their violent opposition to tyranny. Attending college at night was outright dangerous, for Batista's repressive machinery had their eye on young men driving after hours, and I was eighteen at the time. Harassed and searched twice by the police, I was tempted to quit school altogether, since after all, my financial future depended on the family's business and not on Mr. Perez's *beloved career*. Little did I know that my accounting degree would land me my first decent job in the U.S.

Even if I had to pay for tuition, I chose to attend a private university instead of La Universidad de La Habana—a venerable learning institution where Fidel Castro became a lawyer. For years, the prestigious, free- of-charge university became the focus of political turmoil, but since I didn't want to push the envelope any further I enrolled in a private school. In fact, most legally elected Cuban presidents with the exception of Sargento Batista, who had the education of an ape, graduated from La Universidad de La Habana.

Amazingly enough and undoubtedly thanks to my mother's prayers and dozens of votive candles dedicated to La Virgen de la Caridad (Lady of Charity), I made it to graduation.

In order to pay for tuition, support my car, and indulge in things common to a guy my age, I worked at the seasonings manufacturing plant owned by my father and Mr. Albert Johnson, a solid Cuban-American friend.

Of the eighteen workers employed by the company, two were voodoo followers.

How could I ever forget the night El Chino invited me to witness a *bembe,* or santeria ritual, at his uncle's home?

To the beat of drums, participants chanted out

loud to their deities, Chango and Yemaya, for con-
cessions. Then they would cast spells and yell
curses at their intended targets in anticipation of a
frenzy known as *el santo* that eventually would take
them over. Speaking in tongues, they would roll all
over the floor pleading to be heard. Animal sacri-
fices were offered, and it wasn't unusual for one of
the neighbors to find a decapitated chicken wrapped
in red ribbons lying on her portico the following
morning—an omen that someone in the bembe had
cast a curse unto that house.

The experience was so uncanny that I swore
never to attend a bembe again in my life.

At the seasonings business, I was responsible
for developing a marketing base in the province of
Havana, and my clientele jumped from a handful to
about twenty within a year in the meat industry
alone. We began spreading eastward to the next
province and to the next. As the only business of its
kind solely owned by Cubanos, in most cases we
were favored by our kin.

Under Mr. Johnson's tutelage I also developed
additional markets in Central America, all with a
typewriter and telephone. I sold orange-peeling ma-
chines in Jamaica, food coloring in Costa Rica,
electric poles in Haiti, and so on. Half the challenge
was gathering reliable suppliers worldwide, and the
other half was projecting a dependable image to our

distant customers. Even though the items differed drastically in nature, the future seemed limitless.

In all fairness I must also credit my old man for his entrepreneurial spirit. During his fifty-eight years in Cuba, Papa had been engaged in every legal business imaginable: shark liver oil sold to pharmacies as a substitute for the more expensive cod liver oil; smoked fish marketed in areas where refrigerators were in short supply or nonexistent; furniture from Grandpa's factory sold in installments; soy flour for cattle feed traded by the carload; candles of all colors, including my favorite communion white; and toys. American toys I kept when unsold. Oh, how I loved those marketing failures!

CHAPTER 2

The Encounter

Before I get too carried away with who I am, let's take a detour and meet the story's heroine, also known in the privacy of my heart as the woman of my dreams.

■ ■ ■

A cold front is pounding Havana's northern coast with twelve-foot seas and gale force winds that moan and groan as they thrash the water's surface. Facing the wind, some seagulls stand on one leg, others with eyes closed. The air is misty, salt has penetrated everywhere, and it is chilly; Cuban chilly, that is. The Club Nautico is deserted except for some old-timers playing dominoes and their gossiping wives shielding themselves from the wind to make their chitchat more enjoyable. An upper-middle-class association geared mostly to young people, the club offered a white sand beach, boating, weekend dancing to famous orchestras, modern facilities, and two restaurants.

Stiff as corpses, four unknown girls chat at a distance.

"What in the world are they doing here on a day like this?" I ask Tony, Enrique, and my cousin Pedrito—four eighteen-year-olds who are doing exactly the same thing as the girls: freezing inside our short sleeves just because we want to be by the ocean.

"Hey, guys, let's go meet them," I dare to say.

"Four girls... alone? Mmmm, I think we're walking into a trap," says Pedrito. "I'll bet they're ugly as a cough-up, or they wouldn't be all by themselves. But I'll tell you what. I'm willing to take a chance with the tallest if you guys go after the other three. How's that for fairness?"

"Yeah? Then I'll go for the gifted one," I say agreeably.

"Great," says Enrique. "I'll take the blonde."

"That means I'm stuck with the size twenty. Hell, why me?" Tony complains.

"*Mala suerte, chico—t*ough luck, buddy," says Enrique. "Quit being so finicky and let's have some fun."

Trying in vain to keep our hair groomed in the wind, we march to the battlefield. Aware of our intentions, the four girls turn away, chattering and feigning indifference.

"How long have you been a club member?" my cousin breaks in. "I don't recall ever seeing you around. Do you mind if I introduce myself?"

While Pedrito's pitch may sound rather tacky these days, bear in mind that this was the Cuba of the fifties. *Gimmie five* wasn't that cool as of yet.

"Of course I don't mind," replies the tallest one, who says her name is Margarita Minsal. "These are my friends Mariana, Mirta, and Maria Luisa." (The size twenty, the blonde, and the well-endowed.)

Tony comments on how windy and cold it is, Enrique compliments Mariana for her dress, and I stand motionless in front of Maria Luisa, tempted to ask how someone with breasts so big could possibly type anything without making mistakes; but I refrain, for it would have been in bad taste...in those days, anyway.

Maria Luisa makes a few vain attempts to stir up a conversation, but I can't take my eyes off the tall girl in the polka dot dress.

"What a coincidence! All of you have names beginning with M," is all I can say in front of Margarita. Oh, how I wish I had chosen her instead. Seventeen or younger, this brunette is just what the doctor ordered—sexy, tall, charming, with vivid eyes, Castilian-brown hair... and a smile so striking, so tempting...and she moves so gracefully...even her black and white dress is chic. Damn you, Pedrito! Damn, damn, damn!

Later on, Margarita introduces me to her mother, a lady she calls Mima. In her mid-fifties, elegantly attired, gregarious, and very polite, Margarita's mother, a retired teacher from a small town south of Havana, is visiting with a friend who hasn't stopped staring at me since I was introduced. She locks her eyes on mine as if I were a spoonful of castor oil waiting for her mouth to open. The annoying spinster's name is Cecilia, and she has been single all her life.

I recognize her type. Claiming to be virgins, these older *señoritas* ogle men just as one would stare at a dead chicken wrapped in red ribbons lying on the portico. Abstaining from the company of males, some of these "off the wall spinsters" tend to exhibit a holier-than-thou attitude toward men, and it makes me wonder how anyone could go through an entire life without sex.

How can she be so brutal to herself? I ponder with a tad of gentle humor.

Margarita's mother is so pleasant that I wish I could stay longer, but not with her friend around. I've never been chatty with either policemen or chaperones, but being so fascinated by her daughter I consider Mima an exception to my rule.

Two weekends following our encounter, Margarita and I meet again at the club's Sunday dance. My cousin is out of town visiting relatives, and she doesn't have a dancing partner. Blessed be that guardian angel of mine for being so clever.

One of Havana's best known orchestras is playing cha-chas, American music, and everything inbetween, but the rhythms are so ferocious and the heat and humidity so high that we end up sitting snugly atop the veranda's railing, drinking *mojitos* and watching the sun go down.

Cuban mythology dictates that a couple who has met only once shall not sit so close together. Our intolerant Victorian gods, always on the girl's parents' side, look upon us guys with shame and suspicion. But Margarita's smile is so sensual and provocative and she smells so innocently fresh that I say to them: To hell with your antediluvian mores. Put me down in shame, convict me of heresy, condemn me to die at the stake or to hard labor in a Cuban jail, but unless the veranda railing stretches,

I'm not budging an inch.

Either from closeness or excessive heat, I begin to sweat. My baby-blue shirt takes on a cobalt hue, and it seems as though I'm quaking toward cardiac arrest.

"Are you all right?"

"Sure. I guess it's just nerves."

"Nerves? What's wrong with your nerves?"

"Oh, nothing. Perhaps I didn't eat the right thing at lunch."

"That has nothing to do with nerves. Let's go see Mima. She carries Alka Seltzer all the time. I'm sure that'll do you some good."

"No, no. Please don't bother her. It will all go away in seconds. It has happened before."

"Andy, I feel terrible. I wish I could do something."

"You can...talk to me. Tell me about your life. Lie if you want. Here, hold my hand. See how cold and sweaty it is?"

"Nerves, eh?" she says, moving my arm back to my knee.

Wrong move, mister. Wrong move!

But the ice slowly melts, and Margarita begins to talk...and talk...and talk...and I listen, and listen, enthralled, until her father, Martin, emerges to take home his only doll. Unbelievably, at eight PM, it is too late for this girl to be out in the cool of night.

Boy, I think, *what an archaic lifestyle.*

Suitably attired and impeccably groomed, Martin Minsal, a prominent labor attorney, is the kind of guy who never shows up anywhere without a suit. Polished and dead serious about almost everything, clearly because he is also in cahoots with the gods, I find Martin utterly intimidating.

Margarita, her mother, and I walk to the entrance to wait for Pipo, as she calls her father, to bring the car.

"Do you need a ride home?" Mima asks.

"No, thanks, I have my VW parked at the far end of the lot."

A gorgeous, late-model Buick rolls in with Pipo at the helm. *Oiga compay! This girl is not only gorgeous but she's also rich.* I marvel in silence, wondering when it will be my turn to ride in such a hot car. I open the doors to usher the ladies in.

"How come you stopped sweating?" Margarita asks.

She waves from the back seat as the car moves into the night, and I begin to worry.

I'm not in her social league; heck, my parents are not even professionals. Naah, she's too high up. I can't believe she doesn't eat popcorn because Pipo thinks it's bad for her stomach. How can I date someone who's so restricted and stuck up? Nope. I'd better stop before she carries me away.

But then...the notion of Cousin Pedrito wooing her into his web brings my sweat back. Even though Pedrito and I are buddies, we're also viciously competitive with one another.

He's not getting away with this, I think. *No sir, he's not. He'll have to walk over my dead body to date this girl!*

Where did this Margarita girl come from? I will tell you. She lived with her parents and grandfather in a home far away from mine in the suburb of "La Vibora" (the Viper), ten miles from the center of town.

Not staunchly religious, she and her family were true to their faith; thus she had taken all the oaths and gone through all the rituals a nice Catholic girl was supposed to endure...including first communion, with white veil, dress, shoes, and all.

Captain of her school's soccer team, Margarita also had a knack for the arts. She studied piano at the International Conservatory of Music under the tutelage of world-renowned pianist Jorge Bolet. Although she was offered an opportunity to become a classical performer, she declined in order to become a kindergarten teacher like her mother, and she finished at the top of her class in La Escuela Normal (teacher's college.)

Though a wholesome girl who lived by the book, I had never known anyone who attended as many social gatherings as Margarita. She went to parties on weekends and to the movies on weekdays. How she passed with consistently good grades was, and still is, a riddle to me. By now I'm sure you've realized that the only thing we had in common was a family membership to the same club. And that was because I worked extra time to pay the dues.

The next Sunday dance comes around, and as I enter the club's foyer, my *dearest cousin* is anxiously awaiting the girl of my dreams.

"Did you know Margarita is throwing a bash next Saturday and that you're not invited?" he asks.

"Why not?"

"I don't know. All I can tell you is that there was nothing I could do or say to change her mind. I'm really sorry."

His sarcasm is like an adrenaline shot into the wrong artery. Jealous as hell, I don't know what to say or do, short of strangling my relative. But instead of acting apelike, as we usually do under similar circumstances, I slink away with a deflated ego and a heart crushed to mush.

Why has she invited everyone else but me? And what's Pedrito gaining by rubbing it on? Is he planning some sort of scheme?

My suspicions aroused, I dash to the phone to call Margarita.

"She went to the club with her mother," her

grandpa replies feebly.

My self-esteem in shambles, I gaze forlornly around the club waiting for someone to tell me it is all a misunderstanding. That it isn't her fault, that because my phone isn't listed she couldn't get hold of me, that she'll be mailing me an invitation...perhaps a telegram, who knows?

But none comes forward. In fact my despair gets progressively worse as I realize that Pedrito has suddenly disappeared. *Where did he go? What's he up to? Would they be meeting secretly somewhere? Oh, my God, how can I be such a loser?*

Driven by rage, I begin to spread the rumor that Margarita's party has been cancelled—a masterpiece of sabotage done shamelessly and without remorse. *Damn it, if I'm not dancing with her, neither is he.*

Lying in bed that night I realize the cruelty of my plot. No one has a right to do such a thing to a decent girl. And she is so pretty. My God, she's so pretty! *Oh, Adam, you spineless pervert*, I think. *Why did you listen to that woman and eat the wicked apple to begin with? See what you've done?*

■ ■ ■

The day of the supposedly torpedoed party arrives and the phone rings. It's four in the afternoon, and I'm doing homework.

"Who gave you permission to interfere with my gathering? That's utterly sickening!"

Furiously, Margarita harps on and on until the last piece of evidence comes out of her mouth.

"Since you didn't give me a phone number I asked Pedrito to invite you. Didn't he say anything to you?"

"I'll strangle that bastard and throw his flesh to the vultures," I mumble angrily.

"What?"

"I'm just thinking aloud. Tell me, how many guests are missing?"

"None but you, somehow Tony knew it was a plot and told me, so I called my guests, apologized, and blamed it all on a misunderstanding."

My God, how can I be so stupid? Why didn't I think of her first? She must have felt so embarrassed apologizing. And if Tony knows about it, I bet everyone in La Vibora is wondering what kind of a nerd I am. And her father...How can I face Pipo after this?

"I must have lost my head. What I have done is inexcusable. I'm sorry for acting like a mad dog, but deep inside I knew that my cousin was up to no good and to be honest, Margarita, I just can't stand seeing you with that crawler. I know this may sound wacky, but I'm only telling you the way I feel.

Cross my heart."

"For heaven's sake, Andy, there's no point getting mad at each other. Why don't you come over and have some fun? As I said, other than you, me, and Tony, of course, everyone else thinks it was all a mix-up."

"What about your father?"

"Mima didn't tell...I asked her not to."

Seemingly forgiven, in less than ten minutes I shower, dress up, and climb into my VW, which doesn't have enough gas to make it to her home in La Vibora but mercifully does.

Old Spice on a new shirt and Brylcream on my hair, I join the party. The Blaupunkt sound system is at full steam, and as I'm thanking Margarita's parents for their hospitality, Olga, a firecracker of a girl, grabs my hand and leads me to the dance floor, a feat so audacious that Batista would have considered it a threat to national machismo.

"My name is Olga Perez. I'm Margarita's next-door neighbor. What's yours?

"I, I--I'm Andy Ro--"

"Andy, eh? You must be the Andy she talks so much about. You must think I'm loose for what I did, don't you?"

"On the contrary. I'm really glad to meet someone so interesting and outgoing."

Somewhat overweight and petite, Olga's figure

is not what I would consider statuesque. Short black hair, round black eyes, and a red and white dress make my dancing partner the perfect double of Little Lulu. Cute, energetic, but difficult to dance with because of her height and short steps, Olga is fun to be around.

"I'm not as wild as you may think." She lowers her eyes. "Margarita and I are just good friends trying to help each other."

"Oh, I see."

"Is that Pedrito guy a good dancer?"

I shrug. "I'd say more or less like me."

"You do better than I thought...much better. Would you like to dance with her?"

"Me, dance with Margarita? Of course, but that wouldn't be fair to you, Olga. Perhaps some other time."

"I'm gonna make you a happy man tonight, Andy."

"And how's that?"

"Follow me and I'll show you."

"Oops, I'm sorry. I'm really sorry." Embarrassed, I apologize for stepping on Olga's foot as she drags me across the dance floor.

"That's okay. I lost my balance trying to catch up."

"Catch up with whom?"

"Hey, *amigos*, can we switch partners for a

while?" At full volume, Olga staggers Pedrito.

Stunned by her boldness, my cousin bites the bullet and against his will dances the night with Margarita's next-door neighbor. Oh, my goodness, what an odd-looking couple! Pedrito is over six feet tall and his shoes are size twelve.

Ay, Olga, Olga, mi queridisima Olga: I shall never repay thee! Man's power of persistence vs. the frailties of women. What a lovely contradiction! What a wonderful night! Adam...I forgive you.

Olga and Margarita are openly in cahoots with each other. Little Lulu loves to dance with tall guys, and Margarita and I...well, what can I say?

Pedrito and I have been avoiding each other all evening. Tonight we're enemies, and the loser knows it.

Gusano asqueroso, esta vez metiste la pata; this time you messed up, you dirty crawler, I think enraged.

Competitive to the extreme, Pedrito and I are always at each other's throats. According to our mothers, we've been that way since the day we were born.

But tonight is different...tonight is the first time Pedrito and I compete for the same girl. And I can swear by all the Changos and Yemayas of the world that my cousin isn't as crazy as I am for Margarita. *No, señor, imposible.*

Completely ignoring me, Pedrito leaves the party without saying goodbye.

It never fails; the swine is feeling sorry for himself again, I think angrily. *Now our mothers will force us to make up. Damn you, Pedrito!*

A week later my cousin calls to apologize—a routine we've been at for years. "I'm not that fond of her, Andy," he says with an arrogant laugh. "I just wanted to bug the hell out of you."

Margarita walks me to the front gate, her last guest to leave.

"I'll be at the club tomorrow morning," she says timidly. "Will you be able to come?"

"Of course I will."

I get inside the Beetle, start the engine, and stare at Margarita for a moment. She smiles and throws me a kiss.

My hands smell like hers and my chest throbs. I'm about to suffer cardiac arrest.

CHAPTER 3

The Reef

A rusty oil can lies empty on the bottom of the boat for only one reason: to bail water. Free to club members, these wooden rowboats, or *chalanas,* are notorious for taking in water while bucking waves. The speed of the leak is determined by the useful life of the caulking underneath—a once-a-year oakum and tar application frequently neglected because it is such a mess to put on.

I had invited Margarita to tour my *secret* coral reef three miles offshore, away from civilization, police repression, and chaperones. With our swimsuits on and the morning sky shining its yellows and oranges upon reassuring seas, we load the chalana with drinking water, fins, snorkels, and masks, and are soon underway.

I row like a galley slave, and in less than an hour we begin to see the colors of the rainbow glowing beneath the surface. At long last we're over the pot of gold—multicolored live coral formation, a chromatic realm of silent beauty, from the intriguing and poisonous fire-red to a vast number of blues, pinks, browns, yellows, and every conceivable tone in between. My secretly guarded reef teems with exotic fish big and small, barracudas, lobsters, and parrotfish that swim fearlessly between our legs and behind our backs. The water is warm, soothingly warm, and so clear it feels as if we're floating in space—an everlasting space that makes the passing of time irrelevant and imperceptible.

"Andy, please check your watch," Margarita yells every time she surfaces for air. "I think it's getting late. Let's go back before Mima starts to worry."

Where's this woman sense of romance? How can she be so indifferent to natural beauty? And why does she have to be so obedient? I rumble underwater.

"Let's stay a little longer...please! Just a few more minutes, I promise."

"I don't want to upset her, Andy. Let's come back some other time."

Persistence on her side, I finally surrender.

She climbs into the boat, towels hurriedly, and sits in front of me. The on-shore flow is picking up, and we're bucking two-and three-foot waves. Our chalana is leaking faster, and Margarita is bailing water desperately...and silently.

Meanwhile, I'm rowing harder and getting nervous. My blisters are bloody, and I still have a good hour of work ahead. *What if I mess up the trip*? I ask myself worriedly. *This will be the last time we go out on a boat by ourselves.*

And what if we sink? What if I crash against the reef out there, or against that other rock? What if I pull a muscle and can't row anymore? What if we get hit by a squall?

Tired of shuffling so many "ifs," the sneaky side of my brain somehow switches from ugly worries to outrageous fantasies.

What if, on the contrary—I reflect, stifling a smile—*our boat accidentally crashes against that same reef, but rather than making a mess out of things, I rescue Margarita to a secluded beach? Instead of human life there's luscious vegetation, lots of wildflowers, and thunder and lightning all over the place. She becomes so awfully shaky and panic-stricken that I comfort her in my arms. An hour*

*passes, the storm finally dies, and the sun brings its
daily mission silently to an end, and the only sound
I hear is the beating of our hearts and her telling
me what a magnificent guy I am. Ahh! What a won-
drous flight of the imagination!*

"Why are you staring at me like that?" Margarita asks fretfully.

"If I tell you what I've been thinking, you'll be
jumping off the boat and calling Mima for help!"

Damn it! Why does she have to be so cold? I
wonder in silent resignation.

"Would you teach me how to row?"

"Of course. Here, grab this one on my left."

The ice block sits by my side, but not as close as
she did on the railing at the veranda. Briefly confused about who's in charge of its precarious fate,
our sinking chalana circles around until water begins to flow in more profusely.

"I can't row anymore, Andy. My arms hurt, and
I have a tiny blister on my hand."

"I shouldn't have let you do it in the first place.
I'm really sorry."

As I fret about the worst case scenario, she begins to talk, and I'm glad to hear her voice, for it
keeps my rhythm going. "We should be back before
sunset," I say to her. "That is, if we're lucky enough
to make it."

With water now up to our ankles, the chalana

moves much more slowly, and every time we hit a wave another gallon splashes in.

Margarita regards me with wide open eyes.

"Why don't you turn her around and row backwards?" She asks. "Perhaps it won't come in that fast."

"Then we'll be home tomorrow, and I won't have any skin left."

A four-foot wave pitches our boat sideways, sending masks and snorkels into the deep.

"That's my brand new mask!" she cries. "Why don't you go fetch it?"

"Good heavens, Margarita, you're a handful. Why don't you sit down quietly and keep on bailing? Can't you see I'm doing as much as I can?"

Embarrassed, she frets in the back of the boat.

I flush in frustration. "I didn't mean to be rude. I'm sorry."

"That's okay. I know you're in a pickle."

"Of course I'm in trouble. Wait till your mother sees us arriving on a sinking boat at midnight; it'll be the last time you and I go out on our own."

"Naah. Don't be so pessimistic. Mima knows more than you think." Margarita's last words for the next hour or so.

The onshore wind flow tends to increase around noon and subside late in the day, but now it doesn't seem to abate.

I'm worn out, my hands continue to bleed, and my brain is fraught with anxiety. Eyes on fire, the sun rays prevent me from judging Margarita's expression. *Why is she so quiet? Is she upset, is she scared?* I wonder in frustration.

Having faced similar situations before, I am not as concerned about sinking as I am about my inability to forecast heavy winds, my blatant disregard toward her waiting mother, and for not saving her mask and snorkel.

Damn it! I think I blew it.

"Why are you so quiet?" she finally asks. "Are you mad at me?"

"Oh, for heaven's sake, don't say that!"

"Then talk to me."

At that, another wave splashes in. We take in more water, and I get frantic.

"*Ay, Virgen Santa, nos hundimos!*" Hands on her head, Margarita is flustered by the daunting scene.

"Here, let me take the can while you keep the bow on the wind."

Margarita struggles to keep the chalana bucking the waves, and I labor like an indentured servant to lower the water level below my ankles. Finally I take the oars back. *Thank God, we didn't sink...not yet, anyway. Pipo will slaughter me if he sees the apple of his eye—the girl who cannot eat popcorn—*

struggling to stay afloat. I think, beside myself.

The sun comes down faster than I would have thought possible. There's no way we'll be back before it sets.

It is dark when we pull up at the dock. Margarita was absolutely right; Mima is worrying sick. But instead of pitching a lecture, she sees me protecting her only child.

"*Hija mia,* why didn't you help him? Look at his hands. Oh, Andy I'm so sorry. I'll go to First Aid and get you some bandages."

Along with Tato, the paramedic, the good lady returns with a pile of *curitas*, bandages, mercurochrome, peroxide, and even a tourniquet. Oh, my goodness, how embarrassing.

The next time we saw each other, Margarita handed me a gift-wrapped package with a pair of leather gloves and a thank-you note inside. Years later she told me how much she loved seeing me handling a sinking boat. "You looked so masculine, Andy. You actually seemed bigger than life."

Luckily she didn't say it at the time, or I would have crashed the damn dinghy against the reef.

CHAPTER 4

The Evocative Years

Our population divided itself into four groups: the very rich, rich, middle class, and poor, the middle being the largest by a long stretch. Havana's lifestyles matched those of any major western city, and world-class theaters, stadiums, museums, and shopping centers ranked among the finest in the Americas. Our avenues and boulevards were comparable to those in Paris and Buenos Aires, and the most prominent neighborhoods easily matched Bel-Air and Beverly Hills.

African-Cubans and other ethnic groups were seldom discriminated against, and racial unrest was virtually unknown. Our egalitarian society was unique when compared with others in Latin America, where division of classes and racial bigotry still persist. This is not to say, however, that our country was void of poverty and illiteracy, for such afflictions were quite evident in poor areas and in the countryside. In fact, into the fertile ground of both scourges, Castro and his guerrillas planted the first seed of revolutionary dissent.

A tropical paradise treasured by one and all, Cuba has the loveliest sugar-white beaches, turquoise-blue seas, and fascinating geography in the entire Caribbean. From the *mogotes* (karst formations) of the Viñales Valley in the westernmost province of Pinar del Rio to the terraces of Maisi in Oriente, the island boasts having—as Columbus said five centuries before—the most colorful landscapes ever seen by man, a perfect climate with constant sea breezes that keep our temperatures from the sixties to the upper eighties year round... and no snow, for heaven's sake!

Ranging from the unpretentious to the most opulent, 1950s Havana had more yacht and beach clubs than the rest of the country together, offering golf, tennis, dancing, swimming pools, beaches, sailing schools, yacht basins, marinas, restaurants, bars, and everything in between. Entry fees varied from thousands of dollars to modest admission charges at simple clubs that offered the poor a chance to socialize and share in the cheerful lifestyles that made the majority of Cubanos oblivious to our country's most foreboding realities.

Late model American and European automobiles, as well as *cacharros* (used banged-up cars), packed our streets day and night, and Havana's casinos and nightclubs rivaled those in Las Vegas and Montecarlo. But if someone lacked the resources to enter a casino or chose not to, La Loteria Nacional, the National Lottery, came to the rescue every Saturday afternoon at one. Otherwise, *la bolita*—an underground form of lottery invented by the Chinese and perfected by African-Cubans—gave rich and poor the opportunity to lose as much money as they wished.

In the most impressive club of all, the Tropicana, Margarita celebrated her Debutante Ball in 1957. In those days the peso was worth roughly the same as an American dollar, courtesy of the rich uncle purchasing our sugar crop at higher than market prices. Talk about a nephew being spoiled?

But there's always a downside to everything that's good. Batista's repressive reign of terror during the fifties ruined the lives of many innocent people suspected of fomenting civic unrest, especially the young. Widespread disturbances in high schools and universities gave way to vicious persecution, thus saturating my "nostalgic years" with a Satanic blight almost impossible to forget.

His regime about to collapse and morale in the military rapidly deteriorating, Batista resorted to mass executions in a desperate effort to preserve his atrocious dictatorship.

Attending college at night became almost as dangerous as playing Russian roulette with a fully loaded barrel.

My parents never knew whether I would return home in one piece, end up in prison, or in some ditch with a mouth full of flies. I often found my poor mother sleeping on a chair awaiting my return. The sight broke my heart, but other than quitting school and dumping my friends, there was nothing I could do. It was against this horrific background that young men and women supposedly celebrated "the best years of their lives."

In spite of countless scary moments, I never went to prison or visited the torture chamber, although many of my friends did. By attending private schools I always managed to stay distant from young revolutionaries without implying cowardice or creating enemies. But since some of my relatives were deeply involved in such movements, I managed with difficulty to stay away from mutinous demonstrations and subversive acts. Although naïve enough to support Castro's struggle, I refused to participate in public demonstrations, for opposing tanks and automatic weapons with rocks and sticks was not only suicidal, but pointless, given the censored press. Therefore I set my priorities on surviving, finishing a career, finding the girl of my dreams, and looking forward for Castro's revolution to prevail.

To justify my perspective and mitigate a lingering sense of guilt, let's take a fleeting look at December 1956, when Fidel Castro, his brother Raul, Che Guevara, Camilo Cienfuegos, and eighty-two rebels landed from Mexico on the Southern tip of Eastern Cuba at the foot of the Sierra Maestra Mountains in an old sixty-foot boat named *Gramma*.

Relentlessly pursued by Batista's forces, only twelve fighters made it into the thicket. The remaining seventy-four either were killed, captured, or executed. Only during the War of Independence against Spain, a century before, had a small group of men shown so much courage and determination to fight an entire military establishment...and win.

With the help of local *guajiros,* or peasants, the remaining rebels managed to set up camp and eventually a clandestine radio station to subvert the Cuban people. So secret was their hideout that only a handful of men knew its exact location.

My hero promised the complete obliteration of

cronyism, illiteracy, corruption, and torture, the re-instatement of constitutional guarantees including human rights for every citizen, and the establishment of the purest form of democracy Latin America has ever known. The Simon Bolivar of the twentieth century promised free elections, and never in his speeches or press conferences, did Fidel allude to socialism, communism, or any other form of "ism" as his ultimate goal. In fact, the Cuban communist party wasn't even involved in subversive activities.

Along with eighty percent of all Cubanos—rich, poor, intellectual, or otherwise—I became convinced that only a revolution would resurrect Cuba from its ashes into the most civilized and prosperous country in Latin America. Only a giant revolt could eliminate police brutality, demagoguery, and parasitism. Only a man bigger than life, Fidel Castro, could pull the entire country together and rid the Alligator Island of Sargento Batista's black and white trash. All in all, Castro was my champion and I worshipped him.

Only a few persons, like Pipo, who knew the man from the University of Havana, and Don Ramiro, a friend of my father who fought against the communists during the Spanish Civil War, knew, way before my icon's triumphant entrance into Havana, that behind the beard and the camouflage hid a master of deceit, a tyrant in disguise waiting to drive his betraying dagger into the alligator's heart.

In the words of Don Ramiro: "Castro is the reincarnation of Rasputin"—the opportunistic madman of Czarist Russia.

I poked fun at our friend: "A communist government ninety miles from the US? Come on, Don Ramiro, don't be ridiculous."

But Pipo and Don Ramiro were right. Who else but the devil incarnate could transform the entire Alligator Island into an Orwellian *Animal Farm*?

All in all, I can't forgive my foolish evaluation of Fidel Castro—much less mitigate a sense of culpability for taking the criminal for a patriot, for ignoring the wisdom of my elders, and for blindly following the masses. In short, along with the majority of Cubanos, I'm guilty as hell.

But enough therapy for now.

CHAPTER 5

The Ball

Deep in the hearts of the young lived a desire to hold or attend a party at least once a week, either at a beach club or at home, and the most common excuse for us teenagers to spark up a gathering was to rehearse for a debutante ball, a ritual no family with a fifteen-year- old girl would dare miss whether they could afford it or not. Debutante balls offered the pretentious and flamboyant a once-in-a-lifetime chance to make a social statement in which everything from the sublime to the ridiculous was possible, and it gave the poor and underprivileged a unique opportunity to go all-out according to their means.

The popular celebration marked the beginning of an era in which the newly anointed grown-up would be allowed to date, choose a *novio* (boyfriend), pursue a career if desired, consider marriage, and line up priorities. All subject to parental approval, of course. In short, as of that magic moment the debutante was expected to think and act as an adult without the real benefits of such standing.

Debutante balls were all similar in their format. A Viennese waltz danced by father and daughter, followed by fourteen couples, marked the beginning of the event. In modest circles a radio or record player sufficed, and in higher spheres Hollywood productions were not ruled out. Rehearsals took place way ahead of the party, and every single one usually ended up in another bash.

One evening, Margarita and I attended a debutante ball at one of Havana's stiffest, most venerated places of gathering: the sumptuous Miramar Yacht Club, where one of her wealthiest classmates was celebrating her fifteenth birthday. The etiquette: summer tuxedoes for men, evening gowns for the ladies.

The morning of the event I had vacuumed, polished, and added to the interior of my 1958 Volkswagen a whiff of Mother's expensive Nuit de Noel as a final touch. The scent of such a pricey French perfume mixed with the lingering smell of Polish sausage seasoning permeated my brand new Beetle with a stench comparable to that of a pool hall steeped in garlic breath and cheap aftershave.

Worried about the car's distinctive odor and its potentially catastrophic effects, I washed the seats with Ace, a laundry detergent known in the U.S. as Tide, and fanned off the interior for almost three hours without success. My last recourse was to borrow Papa's Chevy Bel-Air, but he needed it for the night, so six hours later, dressed like a penguin, I headed for Margarita's with windows open wide.

I arrived at Margarita's in my aromatic vehicle much earlier than anticipated, for in the Cuba of the fifties the longer the wait, the sweeter the vanity. Mima opened the door.

"You look so handsome, Andy. I'm sorry, but it'll be a while before she's ready. Would you mind joining Grandpa in the library?"

Across the hall from Margarita's bedroom, swaying back and forth in his old rocking chair, Don Luis, her hundred-and-three-year-old grandfather, had just finished reading the newspaper's obituaries.

Removing his thick lenses, Grandpa looked me in the eye.

"You may wonder why I read them, but every

time a friend passes to the other side I cross myself and thank God for allowing me to stay another day." Don Luis had survived a massive stroke at ninety-six, and now he was fully recovered.

He pointed to a chair nearby.

"Please, sit. So you're going to a ball, eh? Let me tell you something son, and I'll be very honest with you."

Leaning closer, Don Luis whispered in my ear. "Dating in the old days was much easier and less trendy than today. None of this nonsense of wearing tuxedos and going to debutante balls in fancy yacht clubs. I still remember taking my date on an evening ride through Old Havana in a rented carriage. Give the coachman a tiny tip and he would stop at a romantic place...I'm sure you know what I'm talking about, don't you?"

"In a way I do, but I'm not sure," I answered uncomfortably.

Looking around before saying something he may later regret, Grandpa mumbled again, "No chaperones, my boy... you understand?"

Don Luis drew a long puff of smoke from his hand- rolled cigar and expelled it in perfect circles above his head. "And I'll tell you something else you may not believe. One fine day, shortly before the sun came out, I took my girlfriend on the first balloon ride ever offered in Havana, and whoo, what an experience that was. The Morro Castle looked like a miniature lighthouse, and so did many government buildings. But by the time horses began to look like ants, my date became so terrified and out of control that the pilot had to bring the contraption down immediately. What a blow. You must understand, though, that I'm talking about the late 1860s. Cuba was a Spanish colony, and Lincoln had just been elected president of the United States."

Wedging the smelly stump between his lips, Grandpa rocked back and forth in wistful recall. The gentle old man had been smoking hand-rolled cigars since he was ten, but never drank booze. "No sir," he said, "none of that kerosene stuff."

Her bedroom door finally opened and Margarita appeared, all decked out in a long strapless chiffon dress, French laced from the waist up, Richelieu embroidered, and randomly encrusted with pearls. Long gloves to the elbows added finesse and her jeweled necklace and diamond earrings a distinctive touch of class. Boy, was she stunning! She looked like a princess...much, much sexier though.

Then the terrifying thought of having to fit Mima and my date into a stinking Volkswagen dawned on me once again. What if they wouldn't enter? What if her mother was allergic to strong odors? My goodness, her friends all had chauffeurs. And besides, how could I squeeze all that peachy

material into such a small car? Hmm. As a last resort I could always remove the front seat. *Oh my
God, please do something! What am I to do?*

"Piiipooo!" Margarita called her father from the
front of the house. "Will you please hurry up? We
don't want to be late and I still want to go for a ride."

"Wait just a second," he answered. "Let me pull
out the car."

Gracias, Dios mio. What a relief! I'm finally
riding in the Buick.

■ ■ ■

Margarita asks her father, who fulfills her every
wish, "Can you drive us to the club the longest
way? The reception begins at eight, so I'm sure we
have time."

The Buick glides through Avenida Carlos III, an
old boulevard connecting most of the suburbs with
the inner city. We pass the Prince's Castle (Castillo
del Principe), an old Spanish fortress perched atop a
rolling hill then occupied by political prisoners, and
reach Avenida de los Presidentes, a four-lane
boulevard split in its center by jacaranda and ban-
yan trees, some over three hundred years old. Finally we cross the Vedado district into Fifth Avenue
in Miramar. The sun is setting, jasmine scents the
air, and it is lovely the world over, especially inside

the Buick.

In an innocent demonstration of affection I slowly move my hand toward my date's, and in no time she pulls it back to where it was. I notice a fleeting smile lightening her features, but it is too dark to pierce it with my fuming gaze. Sensing my disappointment she looks down...and grins.

Boy, is she difficult! I grumble in silence.

Mima breaks the impasse, mentioning the guests she knows will be attending the party, to make sure I don't feel out of place.

Pipo drives through an area of Fifth Avenue where mansions and foreign embassies are as plush as French chateaus—the same buildings that today harbor the top gangsters of Castro's revolution. Where did I get the notion that hard-core communists were to share their self-inflicted poverty with the masses? But I digress.

In a second attempt to hold Margarita's forbidden hand, mine drifts rapidly toward the moving target, surreptitiously grabbing it in the middle of its path. Acting absentminded, Margarita doesn't retract it this time, another proof that nothing beats the power of persistence...even with a Cuban *señorita.*

I'm beginning to sweat. *There must be something wrong with the car's air conditioning,* I think, *or is it my dinner jacket?*

CHAPTER 6
The Production

Afestive mood spices the salty air at the Miramar Yacht Club. The long driveway is busy with parking attendants swapping keys for tags. In the luxurious foyer under the glitter of a Baccarat chandelier, a uniformed escort presents us with evening programs, while another ushers us through the elegant crowd. Margarita greets almost everyone in her path. Pipo is serious as always; Mima takes everything in stride; and I, of course; am on cloud nine escorting a bejeweled socialite.

It's relatively easy to spot among the employees

those who aren't there to serve but to detect suspicious movements, for their crude demeanor sets them apart from everyone else. They are the hit men hired by the host to ensure our safety against Castro's terrorists.

We're led to a table of eight alongside a flower garden and next to an illuminated Olympic-size pool. An older lady chaperoning a young couple sits opposite us. We introduce ourselves and sit down.

Two waiters in tails are assigned exclusively to our table, and I wonder how much seven persons can eat and drink to necessitate two full-time servants standing by.

Sheltered by a coconut palm, our table is a bit too dark for Martin's comfort.

"*Necesitamos mas luz!* We need more light here!" he cries to one of the attendants.

Rolling her eyes, Mima giggles at his unambiguous demand.

Within minutes a crew of three cuts down the branch interfering with the lighting. More than once Pipo had left a restaurant because "I won't eat what I can't see."

Drinks are served. The ambiance is detached. Hypnotized by the empty plate before her, the old chaperone doesn't show signs of life. *Is she breathing?* I wonder. All the coconuts could have fallen on our table and she wouldn't have noticed a thump.

Meanwhile the young couple continues to caress and fondle each other like apes in heat. *Ooops, she's not a nice girl*, I think. *Mine is*.

"They must be picking lice," Pipo pronounces in his deep resounding voice.

"*Calla!*" Mima fires back "Be quiet!"

Suddenly there is silence...embarrassing, ominous silence.

Trailed by fourteen couples, the debutante and her father dance to Strauss's "Voices of Spring." The ball has begun. Girls are wearing white strapless gowns and the fifteen-year-old is clad in peach.

"That color must be in," I say to Margarita, "and if it wasn't for her gorgeous wrap I'd say she looks more like an emaciated ghost. What a waste; all that expensive decoration for nothing."

I'm not through with my unflattering remarks when, after a loud explosion, the ice cubes inside our highballs and Cuba Libres begin to quake.

"There goes another bomb," I say. "Poor ugly girl. There goes her gorgeous party as well."

"Everyone down to the floor!" a bodyguard yells... but no one listens. Tilting our heads as if in prayer is the lowest everyone will go.

Dozens of bombs and Molotov cocktails exploded nightly in Havana, inside movie theatres, shopping centers, and government facilities, under police cars, under any car, in trash cans, sewers, air conditioning ducts, and public restrooms, of all places.

From his hideout in the mountains of Santiago, Fidel Castro enlisted a broad net of underground urban guerrillas to destabilize Batista's government. The strategy was carried out by groups of citizen-volunteers seeking to obliterate the will of the military to fight, and to destabilize the economy by terrorizing the population.

Fed up with his atrocious dictatorship these insurgents were bent on overthrowing the despot no matter what.

Events were rarely cancelled on account of explosions, however, and I never heard of anyone staying home for fear of being blown up. I, for one, seldom missed college at night...or a party, for that matter. In fact, I enjoyed every detonation, because in my mind they came in anticipation of the regime's downfall. Down with Batista! Down with tyranny! Viva Fidel! Bang! Bang! Bang!

■ ■ ■

The emergency generator clicks on and the lights blaze to life, to expose the poor ugly girl crying inconsolably and Papa blotting her tears with a starchy handkerchief. Like mannequins in a store window, the other fourteen couples remain frozen in their spots. Rat-a-tat-tats and bang, bang, bang, but no one wants to leave.

With a commanding pose, the chief bodyguard grabs the microphone. "Ladies and gentlemen, there's no reason to panic. After all, it could have been a transformer."

"Who bombed the transformer?" the chaperone with the vacant mind snaps.

"And what about the machine gun fire?" someone else cries from another table.

"I'm sorry, but I don't have an answer to those questions." Embarrassed, the bodyguard swiftly returns the microphone to the host.

The couple in heat unashamedly continues to massage each other, and I begin to wonder if perhaps they should have been chosen by the terrorists as their target instead.

Without much ado the orchestra begins playing and the festivities resume as if nothing had happened...one more proof that Cubanos have very, very bad memories.

As far as we were concerned, though, the party wasn't a Cinderella event anymore. The enchantment was gone, and so the make-believe. No pumpkins, no carriage, no fun; only terror and the pervasive atmosphere of everyday torture and murder.

The Buick glides silently through the avenues

and boulevards of a deserted Havana, and by the time we get to Margarita's three more bombs have gone off. The mood is somber. No one says a word during the entire trip, and she doesn't remove my hand this time.

CHAPTER 7

The Story of Manolito

What a way to remember her fifteenth birthday. The poor homely girl; God must have run out of pretty faces the day she was born.

It is way past midnight, and mine is the only vehicle awaiting a green light. Five blocks away from home, I see someone trying to cross the street in front of me, carrying a weird-looking artifact. Exhausted, the young man lays the strange object on the sidewalk. It must have been a bike before it was crushed to pieces, I realize.

Narrowing my eyes in curiosity, I identify the stranger as Manolito.

"Hey, Manolo," I yell out the window. "What are you doing all by yourself at this time of night? And what the hell is it that you are carrying?"

"Come out and take a l-look." He bends over from fatigue. "All I have left is a p-pile of junk!"

Slightly retarded, with a speech impediment and the features of a Neanderthal—flat nose, large ears, fat lips, large jaw bone, and high cheeks—Manolito is the laughingstock of the neighborhood's cruel and morally depraved.

Of simple and noble spirit, this guy has virtually no friends, for no one feels compassionate enough to reach him at his level. Infinitely generous and forgiving, Manolito endures humiliation and harassment from policemen and neighborhood bullies alike, because he thinks it's their way of inducting him into the Cuban macho community—a bottomless pool of idiots who enjoy victimizing those of lesser virility. In these times, hounding and tyranny are synonymous with machismo.

"I'm b-biking home," Manolo tells me, shivering from head to toe. "Patrol car stops me. F-fat officer with sunglasses comes out asking for ID. I say I'm not having one. Th-then another cop comes out of car and pulls gun on mmy face.

"'How much did you ppay for it?' he screams in

mmy ear.

"'It was my parents' present for ffffinishing school,' I say to cop with sunglasses.

"'Lay it on the ground right in ffront of the car and leave it there, you mmoron,' cop said to me.

"Then the two go back to car and bbbefore I had chance to scream for help, the ffat cop steps on gas and runs over my bbike, my only bbike, Andy, crushing it to scraps." Manolo lowers his eyes in frustration.

"'This will tteach you a lesson, you s.o.b.,' he shouts. 'Nnext time don't forget your ID.' He sspits on mmy face and leaves.

"'I don't think I'll be sseeing you in heaven,' I yelled at ccop with ssunglasses."

I load the ruins of his brand new Schwinn atop my car and give Manolito a ride home. Sobbing incessantly, he doesn't utter a bad word against the perpetrators.

Meanwhile, I'm mad at God, at Batista, at myself, and at every man and woman on the planet. Everyone is guilty of this *atrocity*—everyone including me for being part of humankind. The incident was so overwhelming, so unfair, so criminal, those bastards, that I wish I had the guts to rally round Fidel and destroy these lowlife gangsters. *They're nothing but barbarians! Yes, that's what they are: barbarians!*

"Thhanks for helping mmme out." Manolo gets out of the car and knocks on his door, eyes downcast, while I unload the vestiges of his handsome bike.

His mom has been awaiting him all night long. Poor Manolito's mother, poor ugly debutante, poor all of us... How little did I know.

CHAPTER 8

La Comparsa

66H*ey, mi socio*, there's a rehearsal at the *solar* tonight, you wanna come?" my friend Juan blares at me from the stairwell. It is Sunday afternoon, two weeks before Carnival time.

"Mama! Do you mind if I go with Juan to a comparsa rehearsal? I'll be back before midnight, I promise."

Detesting my coming home late, Mama's subtle answer is something of a mumble, so I take it for a yes.

Charcoal black, a year older than me, slimmer, and feisty as a mongoose, Juan walked three miles from his house to mine almost every day to play baseball with my friends and cousins against the neighborhood's *mataperros*, street rascals, in a park across the street.

Alternating as pitcher and catcher, we normally ended up in a fist fight to determine who was responsible for losing the game, witnessed by our entire team. To win the brawl one must have his opponent's shoulders flat against the ground for ten seconds. That, in mataperro vernacular, determined who was right in the dispute. And boy, did Juan have a foul mouth!

After rolling all over in the dirt I usually went home to shower. Mama would yell at me for having to wash my dirty clothes, replace all my shirt buttons, and for following the mataperro way of life. Later in the day Juan would walk another three miles to my house just to make sure there were no hard feelings after the scuffle.

"Hey, mi socio, tu nostas bravo conmigo, eh?" ("Hey, partner, you're not mad at me, are you?")

Every time Juan saw me tinkering with my bike, he was the first one to get his hands and raggedy outfit full of grease and grime to help me take it apart and put it back together. Aware of my life's ups and downs, Juan always offered his sincere help in everything but school matters, for my friend was totally illiterate. He also ran errands for the family at 'no charge,' although Mama always gave him a tip or had him join us for lunch or *merienda*— Cuba's afternoon snack.

And every time Juan brought along lunch he offered me half his meager ration, which I humbly accepted, for I loved his mother's cooking. I just wished I had more friends like my buddy Juan.

In spite of their poverty and tragedy, his family couldn't have been more generous, for Juan, the youngest of four brothers had a bedridden sibling who became paraplegic as a result of a car accident. Papa and his older sons labored like mules for miserable pay at the Port of Havana, while Juan worked as a janitor for a couple of movie theaters at night.

Given the callousness and demagoguery of Cuban politicians who unashamedly denied the underprivileged poor their right to learn to read and write, the rate of illiteracy among these hopeless citizens was so appalling that their chances of enjoying a decent and productive life away from the gutter was almost unattainable.

■ ■ ■

It is already dark when we walk into the solar— a dilapidated tenement building with an extensive courtyard in its center shared by all tenants as a cooking area. As Havana's typical dwelling for the very poor, solares usually packed an entire family to a single room, and next to Juan's live an elderly black woman and her nephew, a humongous boxer from whom my friend has learned all the tricks of the trade to beat me up.

It is past dinner time, and Juan's mother offers me *frituras de calabaza,* one of my favorite away-from-home desserts. Sharing so much with this deprived family taught me to appreciate more willingly what calamity came my way, and to this date I still drool every time I think about those delicious pumpkin fritters served with molasses on a hot tin plate.

In virtually no time the solar is choking with relatives and neighbors wearing Afro-Cuban costumes—rich, colorful outfits worn at their traditional festivities during the times of slavery—and with smoke from bonfires kindled to add resonance to the bongos and drums by heating their hides.

Known all over the country for assembling the most lavish and voluptuous display of traditional Afro-Cuban dances, these independent groups of African-Cubans paraded to their syncopated rhythms at the tail end of a long procession of floats, bands, military displays, clowns, acrobats, and much more along Havana's Paseo del Prado every Saturday evening during February—the traditional Mes de Carnaval.

The comparsa tradition dated back to the times of Spanish occupation when, at the end of the sugar cane harvest, the slaves thanked their deities, Chango and Yemaya, for their blessings. Through the years these voodoo rituals became embedded in our culture as an integral part of Cuban folklore.

On Sundays another pageant took place. Late-model convertibles, open trucks, flat beds, private floats, and all kinds of moving contraptions traveled along the same Paseo del Prado with their passengers hurling candy and streamers to spectators. Along with a handful of friends, Margarita rode in a vintage Mercedes convertible, while my buddies and I showed off our ridiculous costumes, hooting wildly from an open truck. *Viva la diferencia!*

Every link to our past, including Los Carnavales, was crushed when Castro took over. Festive signs and songs were either changed to communist slogans or permission to march in the procession was denied. *Cuba si, Yankis no! Viva la revolucion,* and all kinds of garbage in between. By the late sixties Los Carnavales had disappeared from the ruins of our culture.

Two weeks following the solar rehearsal, Juan's huge boxer neighbor is knocking at our door at three in the morning.

"What's going on, Emilio?" Mama asks our un-expected visitor.

"Juan's mother sent me...to tell you..." Emilio chokes with teary eyes.

"Tell me what? What's wrong, what hap-pened?" I ask worriedly.

The boxer stares nervously at me.

"What is it, Emilio, please tell us!" Mama in-sists. "What are you doing here at this time of night?"

"Juan is dead," the fighter mumbles.

A cold sweat runs down my spine. I cannot speak.

"Please, come in and sit down. *Permitame colarle un buchito de café?*" Mother says, offering him a cup of coffee.

Trying to regain his composure, Emilio sits on the couch, Mama next to him.

"A couple of hours ago...a bomb went off at the theatre where he worked," the boxer says, pulling a dilapidated catcher's glove from a wrinkled grocery bag.

Taking a deep breath and wiping off his sweaty brow, Emilio hands me the mitt.

"His mother wants you to have it."

"I cannot believe we'll never see each other again." I clutch the mitt tightly, altogether in tears.

So moved was Emilio that Mama refrained from

asking for details of the tragedy. The black giant stood defeated. I was devastated. Juan's demise was much stronger than the boxer's invincible punch and my macho will not to cry.

Like the votive candle lit at the feet of their St. Lazarus icon, Juan's memory shines on me every time I watch Little League baseball. Ah, those un-forgettable baseball games of ours...But damn it, he wasn't supposed to die that young. No one is sup-posed to die that young, much less so violently.

Precisely one month following the massacre at the theatre, Emilio leaves home for the mountains of Santiago. Loathing Batista and his gangsters with a passion, he decides to join Fidel. The invincible boxer went to fight for his rights and those of his friends and neighbors living in the gutter.

Six months later Emilio is murdered by Castro's own commanders for punching and almost killing a communist in an argument about civil liberties.

"How can Fidel execute someone just because he disagrees with one of his fighters?" I wonder in disbelief. *Mmm...I'm sure Emilio must have done something much more severe to deserve death,"* I think naively.

CHAPTER 9

The Chase

I hadn't seen or talked to Margarita in over four months. What a drought! As an annoyingly persistent guy obsessed with immediate results, I knew she must have gotten sick of my right-now, *ahora mismo* attitude, thus resulting in a relationship cool-off.

By the end of the summer I was already dating a Spanish girl with the looks of a Flamenco dancer. Tall, purely Andalusian, with jet-black hair and penetrating dark eyes, Maria's most attractive qualities were her finely chiseled features, dazzling personality, and a demeanor most men found utterly irresistible. Dating Maria was ego-boosting to the utmost. Neither of us cared to pursue a romantic relationship, but every time I showed up in her company, the men around me flared with rabid stares of envy in which I delighted so very, very much. And that alone, my friend, was worth every nanosecond of our platonic relationship.

Switching escorts and dates as she would dresses and shoes, Margarita also stopped visiting the club as frequently, so for an inexperienced teenager who couldn't entertain the idea of having a boyfriend, she was playing the dating game quite enthusiastically and more expertly than expected.

■ ■ ■

One Sunday afternoon, walking absentmindedly toward the club's restaurant, my mouth drops open as I slam against a girl in a polka-dot dress. *Margarita!*

"*Hola,*" I say eagerly.

"Hola, Andy," she responds, flat as a flounder.

"Where are you going in such a hurry?"

"I'm going home. This place is full of *viejos,* oldies, and I have to study for mid-terms."

"Must you go?" she asks, reddening with embarrassment. "We haven't seen each other in such a long time. Please stay...unless, unless you and your Flamenco dancer are studying together."

Another inconsistency, I think. *She vanished before, so why is she asking me to stay now? Boy is she unpredictable!*

Realizing that this accidental encounter may very well be our last chance to rekindle a stymied relationship, we spend the rest of the evening talking and catching up, and in less than three weeks Margarita and I are shooting the breeze again on the very same spot we first met.

Why keep on waiting? tempts the liberal side of me. *This is a great opportunity! Why not give it a shot, man? I'm willing to bet she's dying for that first kiss. Just propose before Pipo shows up! Come on, this is the finish line!*

Play it cool, m'boy. Play it cool...and be careful, interrupts the boring side of me. *Remember that she's different...consistently different. You're really going to mess things up by pushing the envelope. It's always too soon for her, tooo sooon! Entiendes?*

Torn between obedience and the forbidden fruit, I decide to act like a liberal and go for the apple.

"Margarita, there's something I've been dying to tell you for a long, long time." As I pause she smiles, flushing an innocent pretty pink.

"It would mean a lot to me if you and I ... enjoyed a more serious relationship....What I'm really trying to say is...that I'd like to get a little closer, hold your hand without misgivings. Whisper, 'Ah, there she is, my beautiful novia,' every time I see your picture in my wallet. Do you know what I mean, Margarita?"

All is quiet. To some, silence is musical. To me, I wonder if she's humming my own requiem.

"Not really," she finally replies.

"Let me put it slightly differently then. You have no idea how much I have missed that lovely smile and pretty face of yours for the last few months. Months that felt like an eternity. Now that fate has brought us back together, I can swear with absolute certainty that I was, and still am, very much in love with you. Do you believe me so far? Do you know what I'm asking for, for goodness sake?"

She nods, holding her tongue.

"Then let me ask you something else. If I were the only man left on the face of the earth, would you consider becoming my novia?"

"Yes, I would, Andy, but you're not," she quickly responds. "First, you must accept that we hardly know each other, and yes, I like you a lot. But I need more time to think about that kind of relationship. It's too soon for me. It's definitely too soon."

Assessing her expression and body language, I

understand that my modest proposal has gone down the tubes

"For Christ's sake, girl; why on earth are you so damned difficult?" I say, taking her hands in mine.

Visibly embarrassed, she bashfully lowers her eyes.

Flaring a hurt look I continue to push my luck even further. "All right, I'll make you a deal; just tell me how long I am supposed to wait and I'll promise to be quiet and leave you alone until you're ready. Cross my heart."

"I'm not asking you to desist, Andy, please don't misunderstand me. I just want more time; that's all I'm asking." She moves my hands to my knees.

Facing the ceiling with eyes closed and arms extended, I cry in frustration, "Lady, you're the most difficult...unpredictable...conceited...and...and most dazzling woman I've ever met." *Damn! damn, damn.*

Like that foolish Adam and his forbidden fruit, I become more obsessed with Margarita than ever before. Nothing in this world can be more maddening to a man in love than his woman saying no, no, not yet—with passionate eyes.

In a last attempt to win her heart, in less than a week I'm working on a new plot. Yes sir, a bullet-proof strategy, an absolutely perfect trap from which she'll never escape. Never!

Knowing beforehand she would be attending Sunday's dance at the club, I call on her good friend Tony—the town's billboard—to "share a secret."

With five older sisters, Tony understands the female psyche as well or better than a woman would. A skilful manipulator, he is in cahoots with every girl in the club and handles word of mouth as craftily as a double agent.

"First of all, you must promise me absolute secrecy, for what I'm about to tell you is strictly between you and me and no one else, and I mean no one else...including Margarita. Are you okay with this, Tony?"

"Yes, yes, I am."

"Here's the scoop, my friend: While I have no idea of where and when I may propose to her again, and it may well be as soon as next Sunday, I still need to know something crucial before I stick my neck out. And you, my best buddy, you're the only person who can help me."

"Keep going, keep going." His body vibrates impatiently.

"I know how zealously you guard secrets, and I wouldn't dare ask or say anything that might compromise your integrity. But, *mi socio*, I'll be forever thankful."

"Ask me, please, ask anything you want. Go on,

ask me!"

"Why does she hate me so much?" I shoot from the hip.

"Oh, Andy, why are you asking me such a stupid question? She's nuts, and I mean absolutely nuts about you. Haven't you noticed the way she looks at you? For God's sake, are you blind or what?"

I take a deep, silent breath—triumphant silence this time, for I finally got the big scoop.

You'd better be telling me the truth, Tony, or I'll kill you *si meto la pata*, if I mess up again, you hear?"

"Just trust me. Now, what else do you need to know?"

"I'm sorry, Tony, but that's all. Just remember not to tell anyone, *comprendes?*"

"Don't worry, man, you know me well enough to realize that these lips of mine are zippered. Trust me."

Like hell they are! I think.

Tony's answer must have triggered an adrenaline rush the strength of ten cups of *café Cubano*. I'm ecstatic. I want to jump with joy. What a day!

Sunday comes along, and to set my plan in motion, I ask Margarita to accompany me to the pool deck, for I want her opinion on personal issues of a very delicate nature.

Sitting across from each other beneath an umbrella, she listens attentively to my plight about "how sad I am because my grandfather is dying of leukemia and I don't know whether I should go to Camaguey to see him for the last time or stay in Havana to complete my tests." In fact, to make my pitch more authentic, I present, almost in tears, a blown-up picture of an otherwise true situation. Grandpa was indeed dying of cancer.

Out of pity for my sorrowful dilemma, she takes my hand in hers as we walk back to the clubhouse, where Tony and a bunch of Margarita's affiliates await a signal such as handholding to hail us for becoming novios. So much for '*My lips are zippered.*'

"Congratulations, you two!" they yell as we cross their paths.

Margarita's eyes nearly drop from her head at that. As she looks me in the eyes I note a slight grin tweaking her features, followed by a broader smile sweet as sugar cane. Glancing at our friends we keep on walking hand in hand, smiling casually as if nothing had happened. Like I said before: Nothing beats the power of persistence.

CHAPTER 10

Viva La Revolucion

New Year's Day 1959: (The tyrant is gone! Long live the next tyrant!) Batista, his immediate family, top staff members, and close bullies had just flown to the Dominican Republic in search of political asylum with Rafael Trujillo, the chocolate soldier next door.

Meanwhile, finding almost no resistance from government troops, Castro and his guerillas were walking freely through the streets of Santiago. From a handful of revolutionaries, Fidel's forces have increased into the thousands in almost two years.

Peasants, teachers, military personnel, businessmen, and professionals of all kinds, including physicians like Margarita's uncle Alberto, had abandoned their homes, families, and practices to join the rebellion.

Within ten days, Margarita, her parents, and I are watching the triumphant parade headed by Fidel and his bearded conquistadors roll through the streets of Havana.

It is a national holiday. Soldiers on foot and on tanks, armored vehicles loaded with rockets and bazookas, military trucks crammed with rebels—including Margarita's uncle, Alberto, whom we couldn't recognize because of the beard—all are en route to the country's top military post to listen to the maximum leader deliver his historic five-hour tirade.

Small children wave Cuban flags from their parents' shoulders and older ones from atop trees. Roofs are crowded with euphoric citizens showing welcoming signs and taking pictures. Screams of *Viva Fidel*, and *Viva la revolucion* are heard everywhere. It is anarchy, glorious anarchy. Cuba is free...at last.

Standing on the sidewalk, in the midst of the confusion we suddenly see Fidel Castro parading atop a Sherman tank, so close I could spit on his face—but then in those Pollyanna days I valued our hero as much as everyone else. Everyone else...except Margarita's father, who was waiting for the tank to slow down right in front of us to speak his mind.

"I know that man from the University, and he's nothing but an egocentric lunatic," he screams at the top of his lungs.

"*Callate!* Shut up, or the crowds are going to crush you." Mima tries to calm him down.

"Isn't this a prelude to the perfect state of man? Then I should be able to express myself without fear."

"Pipo, *callate, por favor!"* Margarita implores.

If it hadn't been for the strident noise of the caterpillar treads scouring the asphalt and for the wild roaring crowds, Pipo would surely have met his Creator right there and then.

At the time I thought my father-in-law was acting irresponsibly and selfishly, for he had no right to spoil our joyful anticipation of seeing Fidel, my hero, enter the city like a Trojan horse.

That same evening the maximum leader charmed the entire nation with an endless harangue, during which a pigeon, apparently launched by a smart ass, landed and pooped on the hero's left shoulder, his green military fatigue tainted by defecation. What an omen!

Yet, instead of taking it as a sign of things to come, most considered the incident a blessed symbol of peace—another evidence of the influence of cult and religion in our culture.

By the end of January the union leaders represented by Pipo were fired and replaced by Fidelistas and communist ideologues for no reason other than they were part of the old oligarchy. These dismissals were carried out expediently, with no hearings or proofs of wrongdoing, and in less than a month, all accounts were taken away from him. Small consulting jobs and his personal property were all he had left; thus Pipo traveled from riches to rags almost overnight.

At this time most Cubans, including myself, didn't mind such injustices because "Fidel must have good reasons to be so drastic, and besides, whenever radical change occurs, casualties are unavoidable." I even compared the imposter with Jose de San Martin, the South American liberator, while the more ignorant considered him some sort of Cuban Messiah, or Mahdi, who would bring decency to government and social justice to all. *Viva Cuba libre...Viva Yemaya...*Ha!

Gradually and systematically the great chameleon began to disassemble the island's infrastructure, first by firing and replacing government workers with his own cronies, qualified or not, to such an extent that an illiterate guerrilla fighter named Efigenio Ameijeiras was made Commander-in-Chief of the Armed Forces, and Celia Sanchez, Castro's favorite concubine, became his personal oracle and confidante.

Few of us realized that these ridiculous appointments were aimed at a single goal: the complete obliteration of society and the implementation of a communist paradise amidst its ruins. With no political views of their own, much less social and moral values, these surrogates became easy prey for further indoctrination into the socialist ideology. Give power to a moron and the monster will cling to it like a leech.

But some replacements were not that naïve, and as they gradually discovered the underlying truth, they either quit or mysteriously disappeared from the face of the earth, as in the case of Camilo Cienfuegos, one of the expedition's twelve survivors who was killed in an enigmatic plane crash, the cause of which was never disclosed. A rabid anticommunist, the bearded hero with a charming personality would have become a major obstacle in Fidel's path toward communism.

The system purged itself ruthlessly and systematically in the style of Russia's Stalin and China's Mao until finally all that was left were hardcore communists and hate-mongers.

During this process the constitution was abolished and laws indiscriminately changed, so attorneys like Pipo became the first professional casualties, for most legal precedent was considered obsolete and the principles of Roman law self-serving and archaic.

Trials for so-called "crimes against the people" committed by members of the old regime were carried out like soap operas on TV, and since hatred against old thugs was so deeply embedded in the populace, lynching "by the masses" became commonplace.

Rather than healing old wounds in a civilized manner, the new establishment was seeding new ones instead. *Time* magazine even had the audacity to portray the despot as a Latin David challenging the American Goliath, and when Standard Oil and hundreds of American companies were expropriated from their rightful owners, we cried out loud: *Viva Fidel, viva la Revolucion!*

Assigning incompetent surrogates to manage these confiscations—a disaster of major proportions—Castro took over large Cuban banks, locally owned industries, farms, sugar mills, and large businesses.

To exercise full control of the media, all forms of communications, including periodicals, radio, and TV, were taken over. Commercials ceased to exist, and so did quality programming. Banishing United Press International allowed Castro to create his own Prensa Latina, which was nothing but a censoring organization. American culture, as reflected in music, movies, books, arts, and entertainment, was replaced by cheap counterparts from the communist block. Coca-Cola billboards were plastered over with pictures of communist leaders, and Hollywood movies were banned in favor of Russian turn-offs. Dissention was outlawed, not only as a form of behavior, but of expression as well. Anyone found wearing American fashions, listening to a short-wave radio, or smoking Pall Mall cigarettes, was looked upon with malice and suspicion. Down with Mickey Mouse, Dick Tracy, and Nat King Cole! *Cuba si, Yankees no!*

Our one hundred-and-forty-year-old national anthem became second to the Communist International, and in elementary schools stories like Pinocchio and Little Red Riding Hood were barred, for they were deemed instruments of capitalism designed to dupe the minds of the young. Anecdotes about our national heroes were replaced by stories of Che Guevara as a child prodigy, Fidel as a boy who never lied, and Lenin as the Russian Robin Hood. Blown by the sea breeze, communist trash portraying political gangsters and criminals as role models contaminated our everyday lives.

Books such as Milovan Djila's *The New Class* and George Orwell's *Animal Farm* and *1984* became clandestine best sellers, for they depicted in the minutest detail the communist methodology of taking over a nation. These three books did more to open the eyes of the blind, including mine, than any other form of expression.

Mindful of the Great Deception, in less than a year Cubanos began to turn against Castro by the thousands, and repression went on the increase. The CDRs (Committees for the Defense of the Revolution) were formed and given absolute power over their jurisdiction to denounce and keep track of citizens who thought differently or simply had a mind of their own. Arbitrarily chosen by Castro's Gestapo, or G-2, to spy over neighborhood activities, these CDRs were formed by families whose only mission in life was to spy on the foods we ate, churches we attended, how often we left home, whether the revolutionary flag was displayed on designated dates, and whether we listened to the grueling hours of Fidel's indoctrinating tirades. The CDRs' most important mission, of course, was to nose round private conversations of families under scrutiny. Essentially, the right to privacy and to think as individuals was totally eliminated.

Cousins and friends I played with as a child suddenly became my masters and oppressors, and teachers who refused to impart the new culture were fired or mentally tormented.

Families became divided, those with communist inclinations vs. those who disagreed. Brothers were encouraged to spy upon brothers, spouses against spouses, children against their parents. Teachers were told to question their students about home conversations, habits, domestic issues, and so on. Private schools were also taken over, and everyone blowing a whistle on a relative for not agreeing with the new philosophy was rewarded with even more power and privileges, and accepted into a 'new class' of counterfeit patriots. With his notorious dark wisdom and expertise, Satan couldn't have depicted a more truthful image of hell.

Cuban currency was also changed overnight. The day after the law was enacted, if a person went to the bank to exchange old money, all he or she was given in return, regardless of the thousands or millions on deposit the night before, were two hundred pesos in new currency. Thus all bank accounts were reduced to that amount to force every citizen to work for the government in order to survive. Using starvation and financial disaster as weapons against dissention, the entire population was reduced to equality through mendicancy.

Private property was also abolished. A person could only own one house, which upon his or her demise passed to the government, along with all the furnishings including linens, towels, and garbage cans. Wearing and possessing jewelry was illegal, and therefore punished by law. Any gold, trinkets, charms, ornaments, necklaces, bracelets, rings, earrings, and so forth with any value whatsoever had to be exchanged for the two hundred pesos or less. Those without assets to lose, lost their freedom along with everyone else, and if you wonder what happened to the tons of stolen jewelry, your guess is as good as mine.

Our country's history as written was considered an inaccurate account of events needing further revision. Even the meaning of words like "freedom" were assigned different missions in the newly adopted jargon, and because of the damage inflicted to the tender minds of children during the *Age of Religion*, holiday celebrations such as Christmas were banned from public places and reported by the CDRs as acts of fanaticism against the people. All other religious rituals were viewed by the new class as unfortunate residues of the Spanish Inquisition, and the background music usually heard in elevators, department stores, office buildings, and so forth was replaced by sound systems transmitting a constant barrage of disinformation.

The word "future" as defined in the dictionary did not sound plausible anymore. The entire country was condemned to forced labor and coerced thinking by ruthless fanatics whose only aim in life was to control it for their own sake. Our past erased, the future was nonexistent, and the present not worth living.

At this point let me stress that it took roughly two years for Castro to implement all these restrictions and exercise full control of the population. These events are not necessarily presented in chronological order, for my intention is to offer a view of life under such conditions and not a historical sequence of events.

But two years is a short period of time for such radical change. When the government wanted to distract public attention from these traumatic impositions, an imminent false invasion by the American Imperialists was staged.

"Yankee Warships Sighted in Cuban Waters. American Attack Inevitable!" the news headlines roared on a given morning.

Following the fictitious warning, the regime's next act would be to mobilize the military: Russian Migs flying in formation over Havana, trucks overflowing with troops, camouflaged tanks and armored vehicles rolling through the city, and every single form of communication spewing poisonous warnings of an impending invasion. Even selective blackouts at night were staged to prevent the American bombers from blowing up the city. What a sham!

Also as a result of his contrived states of alert, Castro not only obliterated any residual hopes of future liberation, but legitimized another excuse to tighten the knot even further. Meanwhile the Imperialists across the gulf carried on with their lives and businesses as usual. An invasion, you said? What invasion?

I almost became convinced that Cuba was a huge insane asylum with five million captive patients, including myself.

Overcrowded with dissenters rich and poor, prisons were sometimes used as torture chambers and as anterooms to real insane asylums, where unbending detainees would undergo mental torture in a "scientific" attempt to change their minds; if reluctant, they were left to rot under the most savage and inhumane prison system this side of the Gulag.

In the eyes of the government, the revolution's future was not secured until mind, behavior, and deeply rooted traditions and attitudes were changed among young adults and adolescents. So in order to ensure success in their campaign, a compulsory military duty system encompassing all men and women between ages 17 and 21 was instituted. (Luckily, this new law was enacted shortly after my departure in 1961. Otherwise, swimming across the gulf would have been my only alternative to conquer freedom.)

At the time, smaller schoolchildren had to join the *pioneros,* a pseudo-Boy/Girl Scout-type of organization in which all kids would have the opportunity to learn about the goodness of communism and its leaders in exactly the way it was supposed to be taught. Just as the Jews handed their young to strangers to save them from Nazi brutality, Cuban kids—rich and poor—were sent by their parents to orphanages and foster homes all over the world to save their souls from a certain road to hell.

Their human rights, freedom, and properties ripped off, wealthy Cubanos were among the first casualties to leave Nirvana, followed by the middle class, and ultimately by hordes of hopeless citizens from all walks of life, including the illiterate poor. By the time the misinformed, the unfortunate, and the naïve began to asphyxiate from oppression, leaving the country was almost impossible.

As a last resort to recapture freedom, thousands of desperate families crossed the Gulf of Mexico on small chalanas, fishing boats, rafts and even inner tubes. Many made it to the US, the Bahamas, or were rescued in open waters by the US Coast Guard. Unfortunately, countless men, women, and children drowned, got eaten by sharks, or died under the machine gun fire of Cuban patrol boats, their floating contraptions set on fire to erase evidence of genocide.

Even a few fighter pilots landed their Russian-made MIGs in American territory to seek political asylum, and when the US government decided to ban commercial flights to and from Havana, two determined men managed to escape inside the landing gear well of a Pan Am plane en route to Miami and survived to tell the story.

Hordes of desperate refugees also settled in other countries or used them as catapults to enter the US.

And all this happened within ninety miles of the most powerful democracy on earth. Abhorrent! Bizarre! No question about it.

Since the toughest challenge to the new class was the eradication of all religious and moral values from society—for they were considered the opiate of the people—the self-appointed scholars and intellectuals had enough guts to claim that Abraham Lincoln, Jose Marti, and Jesus Christ were consummate communists at heart, and watch out if you disagreed with such garbage. Unbelievable as it may sound, hordes of Cubans swallowed the pill. There were times when I believed the Devil must have been offered one of those luxurious mansions on Fifth Avenue to help change the shape of our alligator island into a cancerous mole in which every soul would eventually rot in blasphemy.

Reinterpreted and dissected by these forgers, the

Bible was shown to be essentially a book promoting incest, as in the story of Job and his daughters, and megalomania or adultery, as in the case of David and Solomon. And if their mendacity about the Old Testament wasn't enough, how about the sexual relations between Mary Magadalene and Jesus? Amazingly enough, the communists deemed their findings as new discoveries previously obscured by an archaic and self-serving Judeo-Christian faith.

Their second most challenging goal was the fragmentation, division, and systematic destruction of the family unit, which for centuries had been the most venerated institution in the country.

The new dispensers of ideology: Castro, Che, Lenin, and Mao, replaced parents and teachers as conveyers of values. Brothers and sisters were not necessarily such anymore. The comrades of militant affiliations and members of the CDR were declared more suitable to play the role of siblings, because in the counseling of these newly appointed gurus rested the ultimate triumph of the revolution.

In Cuba we have a clear illustration that in communism, humanity has achieved the most scientific, all-encompassing method of taking control of a nation, its mind and its soul; a pure and perfect distillation of all forms of insolence and oppression recorded throughout history, cast into one single doctrine in which citizens, instead of exploiting each other as in capitalism, are instead subjugated, demoralized, and destroyed by the state.

The equality these radicals boasted so much about could only be achieved by leveling every individual to the lowest possible level, whereby personal desires were absolutely unattainable.

In the words of Winston Churchill: "The inherent vice of capitalism is the unequal sharing of the blessings. The inherent blessing of socialism is the equal sharing of misery."

CHAPTER 11

The Story of the Ice Cream Cone

My novia has finally graduated with honors from Teachers' College, but before she's offered full employment in the public school system, she must prove her loyalty to the revolution. Private schools, too, are being taken over gradually and systematically.

Having for obvious reasons changed the institution's name, as well as the names of other people involved, Margarita swears that the story I'm about to relate is absolutely true.

On a Monday afternoon, the lady principal of the Agramonte Academy asked Margarita to show up the next morning for substitution.

Founded in the early forties by Carmen and Ada Agramonte as a small school in the Vedado district, the Agramonte Academy became one of the largest private learning institutions in Havana during the late fifties. From kindergarten to *bachillerato,* or high school, the academy served the city and its suburbs with thirty modern school buses and several buildings spreading over two entire blocks. Children of all races—rich and poor—had access to this private school.

Stern, conservative, and a committed disciplinarian, Carmen ruled the academy with an iron fist. Rarely seen outdoors, she remained secluded in her office, handling administrative matters all day long and giving unruly kids, depending upon their offense and her daily mood, either horrible feelings of guilt or a one-way trip home. Inflated gossip had it she talked and ate through a slit between her lips that concealed metal teeth sharp as Gillette blades. I for one never met the lady, much less witnessed her dentures glowing from inside her mouth, so let's take that as hearsay.

Dressed in black year round and not as cantankerous as her sister Carmen, Ada was the Agramontes' family luminary. Looking as if a bomb had gone off, her office had diplomas and degrees hanging from every wall, and enough papers and objects lying around to bury the woman six feet deep. Kids called her Hada Madrina, or Fairy Godmother, for she offered the academic environment a balance between ruthlessness and congeniality.

But like so many others in the Alligator Island, Hada Madrina suffered from a character flaw. She had swallowed Castro's pill whole and had enough capsules left to push them down the throats of dissident teachers and pupils disagreeing with the new ideology.

No one could believe that such a well educated person, a woman with a philosophy degree and a collection of do-gooder ribbons and certificates of appreciation, someone strongly inhibited by tradition, obsessively conservative, Catholic to the bone, and so modest she never wore color because it wasn't appropriate for a matron her age, could embrace the new gibberish so irrationally, despite knowing that sooner or later her school would be taken over by the same ideologues she worshipped so faithfully. Amazingly enough she didn't care at all about a takeover as long as it was good for the revolution. The woman in black even had her portrait of Jose Marti, one of Cuba's most venerated patriots, replaced by one of Fidel Castro looking amazingly like Jesus Christ.

Hada Madrina's lunacy went so far as to offer the school facilities to the government in the event of a Yankee attack. Overnight the formerly soft-spoken lady of graceful manners had changed into a rabid communist matriarch, and her demeanor had transformed from that of a gentle, reassuring, grandmotherly icon to a viciously brainwashed autocrat. Didn't I say that Satan was vacationing in a Fifth Avenue mansion?

■ ■ ■

It is eight o'clock Tuesday morning, and Margarita is ready for her third grade class. Everything is business as usual until Hada Madrina, filled with revolutionary zest, barges into Margarita's classroom shortly before recess.

"I have a surprise for all of you," she exclaims in a vain attempt to get the class's attention.

"It's a big surprise, children; a terrific surprise indeed, and one you should be looking forward to, so please pay attention."

The kids curiously eye each other, while Margarita stands in a corner awaiting the punch line.

"Someone very important is bringing presents to all of you right after recess. How does that sound?"

The entire third grade bursts into frenzy as Hada Madrina whispers to Margarita:

"Even though you are here for the short term, I expect you to follow my instructions whether you agree with them or not. Please make sure the class shows gratitude to whomever brings the gifts. Moreover, if you happen to find out ahead of time what the surprise is all about, please don't, and I repeat, *do not* tell the children beforehand. Also make sure every child in this room stands and gives a round of applause to our guests. Do I make myself clear, Señorita Minsal?

Margarita doesn't think much about Hada Madrina's request, for it is customary in private schools for companies to bring promotional gifts such as toothpaste, candies, refreshments, and so on as gestures of goodwill, so she eagerly agrees.

Following recess, into a classroom filled with kids awaiting a surprise enters a *mari-macho* woman dressed in military fatigues.

"May I address the class, Profesora Minsal?" asks the woman in uniform.

"Of course, you may," replies Señorita Margarita.

"How many of you children pray at home?"

Most kids raise their hands; others just say we do, or I do, while fewer remain silent. The woman assesses the class, then summons a girl from the front row.

"Will you please stand up and tell me what you

pray for?"

"We thank God for our food and for the things we have, and my mom complains about the things we don't have," replies the African-Cuban girl.

"And what about you?" The macho-woman points at a boy with thick lenses in the back of the class. "Have you ever prayed for the toys you always wanted but never had?"

The boy waggles his head affirmatively.

"All right then, boys and girls; I want every one of you to follow me in prayer." The woman in fatigues raises her hands to the heavens. "Are you kids ready?"

Upon a chorus of yeses Margarita's stomach begins to churn

"Our father who art in heaven," the macho-woman prays solemnly. "We beseech you to bless this class, including Señorita Minsal, with ice cream cones for everyone. Thank you, Holy Father, in the name of Jesus, our Lord, Amen. Now everyone, please close your eyes for ten seconds. One, two, three...

"Now, open them up!"

Taking the woman in fatigues for some kind of loony, the third graders stare each other in disbelief and disappointment, because alas, there are no ice cream cones in sight.

"No ice cream, correct?" She wrings her hands

covetously.

A chorus of no's follows, and Margarita begins to feel nauseous.

"Now, boys and girls, let's make a short experiment. This time we're going to call upon someone else to bring us the ice cream. Are you ready? All right, then; repeat after me:

"Fidel, Fidel, *danos un barquillo con helado*—give us an ice cream cone," she prays.

"Fidel, Fidel, danos un barquillo con helado," the children chorus.

"Three more times please!"

In seconds, an entourage of brownnosers, dressed like jesters and carrying thermal containers, swoops into Margarita's classroom, yelling at the top of their lungs: *Sorpresa! Sorpresa,* while dumping on the teacher's desk enough ice cream cones of different flavors and colors to stuff the entire class like sausages.

Meanwhile the mari-macho woman continues her disgusting harangue.

"Gracias, Fidel, gracias, Fidel. Please repeat after me, boys and girls. Gracias Fidel, Gracias Fidel. Come on, kids, everybody at the same time!"

"I got so sick I had to go to the bathroom right away," Margarita concluded.

It's getting late. Mima and Don Luis are already in bed and I don't want to abuse my "visiting privileges," so I stand up to leave.

"Stay, please stay," my novia interrupts. "I've got to tell you another story from last week. Wait till you hear about this eight-year-old kid."

We're sitting on the front porch, and it's beginning to thunder. A rainstorm is under way. Margarita is nervous, and I sit back down.

"As you know," she continues, "classes usually assemble in single files to recite the pledge of allegiance before entering class. Well, as I'm leading my class into the building, this little boy starts humming the "Voice of America's" theme song. I grabbed him by the shirt to cover his mouth, but it was too late. Knowing the tune, one of the new teachers pulled him aside for questioning.

"But that's not the end of it, Andy. What worries me the most is that some CDRs are pouring sulfuric acid into the ears of those caught listening to that station, and darn it, now I can't get that thought off my mind."

"Look, there's nothing you can do," I say. "It's not your fault, and worrying about is not going to stop anyone from pouring acid in someone's ear. Besides, there are lots of rumors going around."

"I know," she replies. "But you can't say it's impossible."

At the front gate we kiss each other goodnight. Between a bad day at work and Margarita's horror stories, I have enough bad vibes blowing through my ears to keep them numb for a while. I am also tired from frequent nightmares and know they'll be coming back that night.

CHAPTER 12

Business Unusual

Rafael had been working for Northern Provision, Havana's largest U.S. meat packer, since he was fourteen. Loud and passionate about politics and himself, this small forty-year-old mulatto laborer operated the sausage stuffer ten hours a day, six days a week. Though illiterate, Rafael was self-sufficient in meat processing and knew numbers well.

The company's American CEO, Mr. Kant, refused to buy my family's seasonings and ingredients claiming that "nothing could ever match the quality of American products." Nonetheless, I visited Rafael on a regular basis, because one never knew when crumbs might fall our way.

The oldest employee on the packing floor, Rafael resented his boss's arrogance for not promoting blacks and mulattoes. Rafael looked forward to unloading his grievances while we had *café con leche* at the company's cafeteria. In fact, I knew more about the Northern Provision grapevine than any outsider and many insiders.

A staunch racist, Mr. Kant treated every employee without blond hair and blue eyes like humans of a lesser strain. He socialized only with Americans at the Havana Biltmore Country Club, bought his groceries at Kasalta, an American super market, drank Folger's coffee, brewed especially for him, and when ill with appendicitis, he suffered two days of dangerously painful peritonitis waiting for an available room in the Anglo-American Hospital, a clinic owned and managed exclusively by English-speaking personnel. The man would rather have died than lower himself into a Cuban facility.

Other than an occasional greeting from afar, Mr. Kant and I never met personally. The old bigot wasn't going to give a nineteen-year-old Cuban a chance to sell him anything, and even though Father and Mr.Johnson knew his idiosyncrasies well, both agreed it was easier to squeeze oil from a brick than to convince Mr. Kant to give us at least some local support. So bigheaded was this "ugly American" in front of company employees that most felt diminished in his presence.

Then came the revolution and the inevitable happened: Northern Provision was expropriated from its rightful owner, while high and mighty Mr. Kant was given twenty-four hours to leave the country, along with his family and golf clubs.

Due to the straining of diplomatic relations with our northern neighbor and the confiscation of American property, it was virtually impossible for us to import anything from the U.S. anymore, and although most spices came from third world countries, additives, food chemicals, packaging supplies, and other raw materials were imported directly from North America. As a result the INRA (*Instituto Nacional de Reforma Agraria),* or (National Institute of Agrarian Reform) was created by the government, in part to procure worldwide sources of supply.

■ ■ ■

One Monday morning as I awaited my 9 A.M. appointment at the INRA's main office, in walks a little guy in military fatigues, flanked by four soldiers and smoking the largest cigar rolled by man.

"Hey, Andy, *que haces aqui, companero?*

("What are you doing here, comrade?") asks Rafael as he strides in grand procession toward the elevator, surrounded by bodyguards.

As it turned out, following the confiscation of Northern Provision, Rafael was made "comrade in chief" of the entire company. How he managed to read and write during his tenure is still a mystery, but somehow the man knew how to thrive in muddy waters. Just as an illiterate peasant was appointed Commander in Chief of the Armed Forces, and Fidel's lover his personal advisor, the communist government, in its quest to obliterate old attitudes, had chosen an ignorant worker with a malleable mind to run the business, rather than a more qualified employee with a mind of his own.

"Tenemos que hablar lo mas pronto possible," (We have to talk as soon as possible,") he says grandly. "Come see me tomorrow morning at six and we'll meet over café con leche. What do you say to that, comrade?"

Before I have a chance to reply, Rafael disappears into an elevator.

What does he want of me? I ponder.

At exactly six o'clock the following morning, I am asking Mr. Kant's former secretary for permission to enter Rafael's elegantly appointed suite.

"Companero Rodriguez!" the new boss in military fatigues screams through the halfway-open door. "This office belongs to the people now, so you don't need permission to enter. Come on in and grab a chair."

Mahogany panels line Mr. Kant's former workplace. So brightly polished is the hardwood floor that I can see the furniture from underneath. The massive mahogany desk is at least ten feet long by five wide, and behind it a throne-like executive chair three times Rafael's size accommodates the former sausage stuffer in luxury and comfort. Across the room full of smoke, a wall-to-wall bookcase still holds some of Mr. Kant's family portraits, inadvertently left behind when Northern Provision was expropriated.

To the right of Rafael's desk, a set of Waterford crystal goblets stands atop a table and a dozen bottles of the most expensive liquor money can buy cram the glass shelf underneath. A humidor with the world's best cigars gapes open by mistake.

"Andy, please sit down," Rafael says assertively. "How do you like my new office?"

"Wow, Rafael!" is all I can say.

Leaning back on the puffed-up chair, the undersized body of the former sausage stuffer is virtually imperceptible in the tenuously lit room.

"Hey, Jorge, how many times have I told you to close the humidor? Are you a *mentecato* or what?" Rafael snaps at one of his armed servants. "Now bring us café con leche, and don't forget to shut the damn thing on the way out."

On the same silver tray upon which Mr. Kant served cocktails to his golf cronies, Jorge brings us café con leche served in Limoges china. The soldier-turned-servant reopens the humidor and chooses another cigar, carefully closes its door, and snips one end of the *puro* with a fancy clipper. Then, stooping to Rafael, the bodyguard inserts an eight-inch H.Upmann #4--Churchill's favorite and one of the world's best cigars—into his new master's mouth, ignites it with an eighteen-karat-gold Ronson lighter, and slowly tiptoes out of the room. Thus goes poor Jorge, his nose brown as sewage.

Hands clasped behind his head and spreading over the chair as if awaiting a barber's shave, Rafael slowly releases the expensive smoke in attention-grabbing rings, through which he pokes his index finger like a child playing with fire for the first time. Tapping the ashes on the polished floor and laying his boots atop the grand desk, the former laborer begins a dissertation on the company's new policies under the revolution.

His sermon over, Rafael asks ominously:

"On which side of the fence are you and your father these days?"

"On the side that makes most sense...including that of the revolution," I dither, shifting uncomfortably on the leather chair.

"Let me say first that I didn't bring you here for intimidation. You come as a friend because my company needs you and you need my company. Are we connecting?"

"Of course we are!"

"We also know that your seasonings business will be confiscated sooner or later, and that it must be very difficult for you and your dad to participate in its extermination. However, in light of the inevitable and provided you put your heart to work for the common good, I'm willing to make you an offer."

"And what kind of a deal is that?" I ask, trying to keep my voice even.

"Because of our difficulties obtaining American goods, would you consider matching every seasoning and ingredient previously acquired from the Imperialists and supply them to us, blended and packaged in the same manner?"

I nod cautiously. "And what do I get in return? Starvation?"

Rafael frowns and sits forward. "Don't get sassy, Andy. Let me finish. First of all, I'm willing to offer you my contacts with the INRA to facilitate the importation of goods from the Eastern Bloc. Then, as soon as the government confiscates your business, I promise to find jobs for you and your dad right here at the packing house. I can't guarantee what kind of work you'll be doing, but your friend Rafael will do everything possible to help the two of you earn a living...a very modest one, that is.

"I also realize how unpleasant it must be to give up a good way of life after years of hard work, but hopefully my offer will make you feel much better. In the end it's all for the common good, and of course for the revolution. And please don't misunderstand me. I'm not threatening you. I'm just trying to be as fair as I can under the circumstances. Do you understand? What do you say to my generous offer?"

I gnash my teeth and clench my fists in anger. My face is hot and my spine sweats. Like a lizard on the prowl, Rafael has new colors. The human chameleon is about to clench his jaws on my jugular and bleed me dry.

No metas la pata, Andy, cool off before you say something foolish, my cautious side thinks in miserable resignation.

"I understand perfectly well. I also know where you're coming from, and I have no other choice but to cooperate."

"That's great then! You'll hear from me or my secretary within the next couple of days."

Your turn will come, you miserable bastard!
I think, infuriated.

Rafael stands. "Jorgeeee! Come into my office

and walk Senor Rodriguez to the front door."

"Andy!" He winks at me as I cross the threshold. "Perhaps you'll become a good communist after all...who knows?"

Back in the office, I don't say a word about the meeting to anyone, including Papa. I'm so embarrassed and humiliated by that fool's arrogance that I decide to save everyone else the demoralizing effect of total subjugation, at least for the time being. Of our company's fifteen employees, five are relatively poor but literate, and every single one loathes communism with a passion.

Three years following Rafael's appointment to Chief Comrade of "Embutidos Cubanos," formerly Northern Provision, the fifty-year-old company permanently closes its doors because of irreversible shortages.

A year later, a good friend of mine tells me that Rafael was eventually demoted to "volunteer comrade" of a sugar-cane cutting crew. Back to the trenches and to the grindstone, my stupid friend! Once you dwelled in arrogance; now you sweat and smell like an ass. Poor Rafael.

CHAPTER 13

Decisions, Decisions

It's four A.M. and I'm in bed arguing with my liberal and conservative sides about the future. A dark, unpredictable, and meaningless future; a futureless future, to be precise. Cuba is hopeless, no question about it.

"Would you consider it stupid to wait much longer to cross the gulf?" I ask both sides.

The liberal side firmly replies:

"Do you want to build your home in hell? Would you be happy seeing Margarita in rags the rest of her life, as well as your children? Would you let Fidel raise them? Would you like to become an automaton instead of a surgeon, or an accountant for that matter?"

"No," I admit to myself. "There has to be a way out, a means to recapture hope, don't you think?"

"That's precisely what I'm trying to say, Andy. The answer is across the gulf, my friend, or else stay and forfeit the past, the present, and the future forever."

"Right across the gulf, you say? Can't I wait a little longer before deserting my beautiful country?"

"Cross the gulf or lose your humanity!" chimes in the conservative side. "Hell, Pedrito is already on the way out. Do you mean to tell me he has more guts than you...or does he?

"When your father left Nuevitas for a better future in Havana the man didn't have a penny cut in half, and he made it. Didn't he?"

"Yes sir," I agree, "my old man made it."

"Then why can't you? After all, you're his son. Look at it this way: if the seasoning business is doomed and there's no private enterprise, how can you survive as an accountant? If you're going to slave for the government here, why not find a job with a future somewhere else?

"And we're not talking only about your financial future, Andy. This is about becoming human again, about reclaiming your life, your soul... her soul...and the soul of your children."

"Do you see our point now?" both sides say in unison.

"What about Margarita's parents?" I ask. "What about mine?"

"If you leave alone you'll lose her. But both will lose everything if you stay."

"Are you suggesting we get married and get out?"

"Of course, dummy! That's exactly what we're saying," both sides pronounce simultaneously.

"Then why wait? *Que diablos*, I'm proposing to her right now. You guys have got me convinced."

"You were born in a hurry, Andy, and you'll never change, that's all I can say," Mama says at breakfast the following morning.

"Didn't you and Papa leave Nuevitas to find us a better future in Havana? How would you like to see your grandchildren raised in this cesspool? Of course I'm in a hurry, wouldn't you be?"

Mama fixes me with a compassionate gaze.

"Go tell Margarita that you love her and that you cannot leave her behind. Tell her exactly what you told us and make sure she understands." She turns to my father. "Well, Andres, how about you? Do they have your blessings as well?"

"Of course they do," he answers worriedly. "I just don't think it's the right time to rush into that kind of venture."

Mother had the patience of an oyster and the temper of an operatic diva. Hair white as chalk by the time she was thirty, she became queen of the San Juan Festival (local carnival) in her home town of Camaguey at age twenty. Not only was she a beautiful woman but very gregarious and compassionate as well.

At work that day, everyone is talking about an impending CIA-sponsored invasion to get rid of Fidel Castro. Meanwhile, my sleep-starved brain continues to choke with imponderables.

How can I propose so quickly without sounding recklessly impulsive? What if she says no? Goodness, if it took her six months to become my novia, how long will it take her to deal with a marriage proposal?

"Why ponder so much about it? Can't you see your butt is on fire? Call her right now, for Christ's sake!" says my liberal side.

Our phone conversation goes from small talk to a void. My worst fear is getting a no for an answer and it's beginning to look that way, so I go straight to the point.

"There's something very important I want to talk to you about. Is there any way I can see you privately?"

"Sure, drop by this afternoon. I'll be alone while Grandpa is in the library. But what's all the secrecy about? Is there anything wrong? Are you and I okay?"

"Everything is better than okay, Margarita. I'll see you after lunch."

No *almuerzo* that day. My stomach has been curdling for twenty-four hours, and food is the last thing it needs. All I want is a yes.

At two in the afternoon Margarita and I are sitting on the front porch facing each other.

"You're sweating like a sponge. Is everything all right? You look so worn out, Andy. How about some ice water?"

"No, thanks."

"Aren't you supposed to tell me something?"

"Yes. I'm considering..."

"Then say it."

"I want to marry you," I say with trepidation.

Margarita stands up as if the chair is on fire.

"Well, so do I," says the girl in my favorite polka-dot dress...smiling.

Stupefied, I take her hands in mine. *She must think I'm joking*, I wonder at a complete loss.

"I'm not kidding, Margarita. I'm dead serious. Let's get married as soon as possible."

"I'm also serious," she says decisively. "In fact, Mima and I already had a talk."

"What did she say?"

Back on her seat, Margarita looks deep into my

eyes and whispers:

"Is he a good Catholic, do you like him? Are you in love with him?" My novia clings tightly to my hands.

"And your answer-?"

"Yes he is, yes I do, and yes I am."

"Then what happened?"

"She tells me that because you were a *Fidelista* until recently, Pipo doubted your ability to make good judgment. But then she goes, 'Don't worry, *hija mia*, go after your heart and follow him. I'll take care of your father.' Those were exactly her words.'"

"And what was your reaction?"

"I expressed disappointment about the way Pipo felt and that I wouldn't be having the kind of wedding I always wanted."

"'The important thing is whether you're willing to sacrifice everything for him,' Mima continued. 'If your answer is yes, then let your father and me worry about the wedding. We'll manage somehow. And remember; when God closes a door He opens a window.' Then she hugged me with teary eyes."

My bride looks radiant—a glow visible from the heart for eyes alone cannot capture the splendor of the moment.

I kiss her on the cheek—another "thou shall not" in Cuban porticos during daylight.

"*Ay, Dios mio*, what would the neighbors think of me?" she exclaims, panic-stricken.

The grand day is tentatively set for the summer of 1962—two years away.

"Whenever Andy comes," Mima often complains, "he moves the wedding day up another notch. When is this going to stop?"

Living up to my reputation, the following week I show up with the wedding ring.

Finally, on the afternoon of November 26, 1960, almost two years ahead of schedule, with an elegant but simple ceremony at the Corpus Christi Catholic Church in Miramar, we take our marriage vows.

Margarita's wedding dress has been especially designed by Angelita Novias—the most reputable fashion designer in Havana and a close friend of the Minsals. Holding a fresh bouquet of orange blossoms and Spanish daisies (margaritas) my bride walks up the aisle with irresistible bashful eyes, her slender figure sexier than ever. She looks stunning.

I sweat like a sponge waiting for Pipo to hand me the apple of his eye. *Damn, is so hot inside this suit!*

The ceremony begins, and I lose track of who is saying what until Margarita drives her right elbow into my ribs.

"Yyes, I do," I stammer.

The ceremony over, my bride and I stride

slowly to the entrance, where a chauffeured limousine awaits to take us back to her parents' home for the reception.

From the back of the front seat hangs a large spray of gardenias. I snatch a blossom and offer it to my wife. Holding it in her hands we glance at each other in disbelief.

My, God, what have I done? I wonder as we glide through town.

The black Cadillac pulls up at the curb, and the party begins. Attending guests, about fifty.

Workers from the Bakers Union, one of Pipo's former clients, have prepared for the "lawyer's daughter" an intricately decorated wedding cake. A meringue architectural masterpiece.

Parents, friends, company employees, two of Margarita's former nannies, my cousin Luisita, Aunt Ana Maria, their chauffeur Jaime, carefully selected neighbors, and people I'd never seen before, form our modest guest list. I would have invited Pedrito, but by then he had already left the country.

Kids drink punch, everyone else wine and cocktails. Cecilia, the spinster, sits in a corner slurping café con leche with a widow-friend. With walls on both sides she feels secure, for contrary to Cuban mythology walls don't have ears. Old Cecilia doesn't give me a foul look this time.

I guess I'm not a male prowler anymore, what a dispensation! I reflect a tad wickedly.

At least four times I visit the bar for mojitos. I need to decompress. Friends are driving me crazy, and there's so much rattle inside the house that the CDR spy on call must think it is gasping for air. Cubanos are loud, emotional, and *divertidos* (fun seeking), and no matter how bad things are, parties are always parties.

Tony—the town's billboard—ties a line with empty cans to the rear bumper of my VW (an American tradition), and Victor, a close friend, makes sure there's enough rice to fill up our ears on the way out. After changing into more conventional outfits, we're ready to take off on our honeymoon trip...*recien casados, al fin!* Wedded, at long last!

Inside the car, happily hitched and with glee to spare, I'm still hostage to some sort of floating anxiety that's been on me for quite some time—a vague feeling of urgent anticipation that darkens the colors of life as I think of the uncertainties of trials to come.

Born with unflinching faith and a rose-colored lens, Margarita seldom feels apprehensive. She is optimism incarnate—unsullied, uncorrupted, and exquisitely naïve.

CHAPTER 14

The Honeymoon

The revolution's wedding present arrived a day before the ceremony—a letter allowing us ten days to remove our personal belongings from our business premises. We were scheduled for confiscation the first week of December.

This wasn't what anyone would call a propitious beginning for a marriage. Being the owner's son marked me as a prime target for termination, and the fact that I'd be assigned to work for another buffoon like Rafael worried me to no end. I also knew that timing and momentum were on my side, but unless I acted aggressively my other alternative would be inner-tubing across the Gulf of Mexico as a single man, for Castro was insidiously tightening the noose around those despising the brutality of his regime.

On pins and needles Margarita and I started our week-long honeymoon. First stop: the luxurious Capri Hotel downtown. After all, why not live it up before destitution?

Next morning we called for room service: an American-style breakfast of bacon, eggs, pancakes, you name it. No pan, mantequilla y café con leche, as most Cubanos usually have. Suitable dressed for a trip to the country, Margarita wore brown hiking boots, khaki pants, and a fitted white blouse that made her waist look even smaller than on the wedding gown, and just a little make-up, which I liked.

Dressed in a similar outfit but with a white shirt, I looked more like a clone than a husband.

We were to drive five hours through the country's most spectacular scenery en route to the Viñales Valley, our final destination and one of the most beautiful spots in the Cuban countryside.

"Don't you feel strange without a chaperone?" she asked blithely.

"I'd say it's a bit new, but nevertheless a wonderful experience." My arm around her shoulder, I kissed her on the cheek.

She panicked as the Beetle briefly swayed to the

edge of the road. "*Ay, Virgen Santa, nos estrella-mos!*" "Holy Mary, we're going to crash!"

An early winter rainstorm the night before had left a sweet smell of dampness and a false sense of spring. The greenery was breathtaking, and I had never seen more royal palms clumped together in my entire life. Stop after stop I asked the same question.

"Will we ever see our country again? God knows how much I hate to leave this place."

"Of course we will, silly, don't be such a pessimist," my cheerful wife always replied.

Studded with peasant huts, or *bohios,* a rural scene of stunning beauty and vitality unfolded before our eyes. One of the few *karst* formations in the world besides China's Giulin Valley, Viñales, with its rounded knolls called *mogotes,* offered a magnificent background to the thousands of orange and purple flowers bursting from the jacaranda trees below our hotel balcony.

Strategically perched upon a hill overlooking the Organos Mountain Range and the amazing valley itself, the Hotel Los Jazmines—a magnificent example of colonial architecture—was one of the few paradisiacal locations left unscathed in the tormented Alligator Island.

Touring the countryside we saw how the world's best tobacco plants were cared for one leaf at a time before they were dried, bundled, hand-rolled, packaged in cedar boxes, and sold to the British prime minister for ten bucks a stick—or given to Rafael for free. Sir Winston sharing the world's best cigars with a fool like him? How irrational, how ludicrous, I thought. What a joke!

Our honeymoon is in its third day, and Margarita and I are having dinner on the main terrace. Enchanted by the setting, she's lost in thought. Falling to her shoulders, her soft curls ebb and flow in the gentle breeze. I glance at her. With well-defined lines, the new dress is sharp, colorful, revealing...Boy, she's so striking!

Silver-plating the entire valley, a full moon makes the cozy bohios stand out like diamonds in the rough. The air smells of gardenias, the skies are transparent, the mockingbirds and the *trogones* are still, and we're the only ones enjoying such a lovely evening outside.

"Señor Rodriguez, you have a message from Havana." A bellman hands me a scented yellow envelope with a card inside. I'm scared stiff— *Something terrible must have happened.*

Los Jazmines does not have room phones, so messages are intercepted by the hotel's operator, scrutinized by a resident stoolie, and passed to the guest via the bellman—an innovative way of wiretapping our personal lives. *Viva la Revolucion!*

"Open it. It may bring good news from home,"

says Margarita.

I frown and shake my head. "Father wouldn't have done this unless something really bad happened."

"Go ahead and open it. I'll bet it's good news," my bride says confidently.

This is it. *Now we're all out of work*, I think in despair, overwhelmed with fear.

I tear open the envelope and read its contents with shaky hands:

The business is ours until further notice. Big Brother changed mind...temporarily. Have a great time. Papa.

At that moment on the hotel's terrace, I imagine how a patient given a death sentence would react to news that he was diagnosed with the wrong disease. The comparison may sound preposterous, but the reprieve feels as dramatic to me.

In celebration we order the last bottle of Rioja Marques de Riscal in stock, and following dessert I ask the waiter for an H.Upmann No.4.

Five days later we drive back to reality—Margarita's home until further developments.

A cold front is passing over. It is cloudy, windy, and cool. The countryside looks dreary, the green has turned gray, and it smells of hard times.

"Is life only a state of mind?" I ask.

"Who cares, Andy? Stop thinking so much."

CHAPTER 15

Cousin Luisita

Her chauffeur is knocking on our door. It's early in the morning on April 16, 1961, one day before the "Great Deception."

"La señorita would like you to join her for a ride," says Jaime, looking smart in his black uniform.

"Of course, tell her I'll be out in a minute," I reply.

Every time my cousin Luisita comes to Havana, she shows up unexpectedly in her chauffeured black Cadillac. Our personalities are opposite but the chemistry is perfect, so I always look forward to seeing her. This time, Margarita is out of town with her mother.

Coming from a very wealthy family, my oldest cousin, at twenty-six, has been all over the world. Educated in Montreal's most prestigious school for *señoritas,* she has a philosophy degree in Religious Studies, a Master of Arts, and speaks four languages fluently, including Latin and Greek. Uniquely attractive, Luisita's personality, education, and refinement make her worthy of a royal. Impeccably dressed by Parisian couturiers, she always makes a statement wherever she goes.

Today, Luisita is wearing a black pant-skirt, sandals, a white turtleneck, and her inseparable piece of jewelry—the Rolex watch presented by both parents upon graduation.

"What in the world are you doing here so early?" I ask my dearest relative and trusted confidante.

"Uncle Guido thinks the U.S.-backed invasion is about to begin. I wanted you to be the first one to know that American warships are on full alert, and Kennedy has promised to darken the skies with fighter jets, and Guido's cell (subversive group) is ready to blow up three police stations as soon as the invasion takes hold."

"Slow down, slow down!" I say, holding up a

hand. "Just think about it. If Guido, you, Jaime, and I know what's going on, don't you think the government does?"

"It's all being handled by the CIA, and that's good enough for me," she asserts.

She taps the chauffeur on the shoulder. "Jaime, will you take us to the Recodo Guarina for lunch and then to La Puntilla?"

I smile. We're going to a famous Cuban-American hot-dog stand, and to a black reef north of Havana where the ocean deposits unusual mollusks and shells on every tide.

Knowing that her chauffeur of twenty years always keeps towels handy in case she gets sprayed, Luisita likes to sit as close to the water's edge as she can to breathe the salty mist from the crashing waves. Sitting on a small cushion, she reads books or writes poetry while Jaime, with the patience of a clam, gathers and classifies exotic shells for his collection.

Too early for hot dogs, we stop at the sharp-edged reef of La Puntilla to watch the sky-blue waves crash against the jagged rocks.

"Did you know I was once tempted to become a nun?" she asks me with a wry grin.

"My favorite cousin: A nun? You've got to be kidding."

"Why not? Ever since the day of creation, humankind has tried to reach a higher power. Whether we worship a rock, a statue, the heavens, or a deity of some kind, we're all pursuing the same thing: a sense of wholeness and peace. Internal peace, spiritual peace, whatever you want to call it. And to tell you the truth, the only time I have experienced something like this was during my boarding school years in Montreal."

"A religious experience, eh? Why didn't you tell me?"

Because I thought you'd laugh at me. You see, for some mysterious reason every time I visited with Sister Gloria, I felt so serene and peaceful in her presence that I always wondered if it was God's way of calling me to his service. This was a daily occurrence throughout my seven years of college. Sister Gloria and I still write to each other, and she always tells me that there are other ways to serve the Lord besides becoming a nun."

"You want to know something?" I say openly. "Now, more than ever, I appreciate having a woman in my life. Someone I can trust, love, fight with, fight for—a close friend to share the rest of my life with. Look at priests, for heaven's sake...no family, no intimacy. Only God and Jesus, day in and day out!

"Sister Gloria must have had good reasons to discourage you, don't you think? A nun...good heavens! How can you live without sex the rest of your life? Did you ever tell your parents?"

Luisita lowers her eyes, embarrassed.

"I should have said it more gracefully. I'm sorry."

"Papa adamantly opposed it, and Mama blamed him for sending me to a religious school so far away from their influence. So you see, I was already in trouble."

"Do you regret it now?"

"Sometimes I do, especially when I think it could have been my vocation. That's the reason I dedicated my life to philosophical and religious studies. So many degrees and accolades for nothing! No matter how much knowledge I acquire, how many holy places on earth I visit, or how many times I pray for that same sense of oneness to recur, I still have that vacuum inside, longing to be filled."

"Why don't you go back to Montreal?" I suggest. "Spend some time with the nuns, visit with Sister Gloria, and ask yourself the fundamental question: 'Is this really for me? Would I be happy wearing a habit and leaving everything behind, including family and friends, to become a recluse the rest of my life?' Suppose that feeling of peace you're talking about wears off with time; then what?"

Stroking an empty shell, she examines it in pensive recall.

"I don't know, Andy, but I'll tell you this much; if I ever experience that stillness of heart, mind, and spirit again, I'll leave everything to keep it."

"Including Alfonso? Didn't you say the two of you are very much in love?"

"That's my other dilemma, in fact my biggest one."

"Then go back to Montreal, for Christ's sake, and decide if that's what you want to do. Be honest with yourself and with Alfonso. Ask him to give you a month or two to make up your mind, and if after all this soul-searching you still want to get married, by all means do it in Montreal."

"You know, I think that's an excellent idea." Smiling, she wrings seawater from the base of her skirt.

Luisita decided to go to Canada and spend a month with the sisters. Knowing she would need money while there, she traded some of her jewels for U.S. dollars through a trusted cell, which in turn deposited it at the Royal Bank of Canada in my cousin's name, pending her arrival.

Naively enough she mentioned the successful maneuver to her sister-in-law Alicia—an under-cover *chivato* (agent) no one in the family knew about.

The resentful conniver blew the whistle to the CDR, and as Luisita was boarding the plane to

Montreal, she was arrested and tried by a "people's tribunal"—a lynch mob with a fancy name—found guilty of treason, and sentenced to hard labor for life.

Alicia was promoted to a higher rank in the spy world, and Mario, Luisita's spineless brother, was disowned by the entire family for not standing up to his betraying wife. Unable to handle the guilt and shame, Mario filed for divorce and escaped to an unknown land in a Spanish cargo ship. No one has ever heard from him; hopefully no one ever will.

Twenty years into her agonizing prison term, mentally and physically wasted, my religiously devoted cousin—abused and tormented by her captors—developed terminal breast cancer that was purposely neglected by her guards to make her suffer "like your s.o.b. Jesus Christ did."

In order for Luisita to marry her life's one and only love before the inevitable, Aunt Ana Maria contacted the Pope to intervene on her behalf. The pontiff succeeded, and she was released to marry Alfonso. Three months following the wedding, Luisita passed away, free of bondage at last. Poor Luisita.

CHAPTER 16

A Day of Infamy

How could I ever forget the fateful morning of April 17—one of my life's saddest.

"Andy, Andy!" Margarita barges into our room. "The invasion has landed and the insurgents have taken control of a beach. Your mother just called on the phone."

"How does she know?"

"From the short-wave radio; come on, let's listen to it."

Armed with the latest combat equipment,

backed by U.S. planes, and joined by thousands of locals, a brigade of heroic volunteers is making headway into the Bay of Pigs in an effort to free our country from communist thugs. A la marcha, cubanos valientes! El Presidente Kennedy has personally expressed his support, and the underground is already carrying out their missions. It won't be long before Cuba is free again! Viva Cuba Libre! Abajo el comunismo! Bla, bla, bla...the news from Insurgent Radio.

"You haven't heard the local station, have you?" Felicia, our next-door neighbor, dashes in, eyes full of tears. "They are arresting thousands of suspects and holding them hostage in theaters, stadiums, and public buildings. Worst of all, my brother-in-law, Felipe, is among them, and he has nothing to do with the invasion. It's a mess out there, my friends. It's a big mess."

Butterflies in my stomach, I turn the dial to a government station. Mima is back from the kitchen.

This morning, in a fruitless effort to depose our popular revolutionary government, a group of resentful Yankee lackeys armed with obsolete WWII weapons and backed by two B-26 bombers made a foolish attempt to capture a beach-head in the Bay of Pigs. In a matter of hours our courageous militia had recaptured the area, and right at this moment, our maximum leader is inspecting the battlefield.

"Someone's lying." Felicia wags her finger madly at the radio.

"Where's your father?" I ask Margarita.

"Back in the shop listening to the Voice of America. He thinks they're more reliable."

She shouts from the hallway:

"Piiipooo...please come over, we want to talk to you!"

Eyes downcast, Pipo stands solemnly in front of Margarita and me.

"Bad news," he says. "Kennedy has abandoned us. Fidel has won and the invasion is over, so you two must leave the country, for I will not allow my grandchildren to be raised in this sewer."

Mima takes a seat without saying a word, and Margarita and I gaze each other in disbelief.

I grab the phone to speak with my father.

"Whether we lose everything or not," he tells me, "Mother and I are leaving Cuba as soon as possible. This madman has made a pact with the devil, and things will be getting much worse from now on. We're--"

"Perhaps Kennedy will send the Marines," I interrupt in a foolish attempt to calm him down.

"Are you kidding? The Russians have scared him by invading Berlin, and that's why he's chickened out. The Bay of Pigs was nothing but a sham and a tragedy to us, and as far as I'm concerned, this is the end, Andy. It's over, period."

What an awful day, pervaded with terrible feelings of hopelessness and gloom. What a night to make decisions, juggle contradictions, understand paradoxes, and question the Lady of Charity for allowing evil to prevail.

I keep hearing Pipo telling Margarita to leave the country, for he doesn't want his grandchildren "raised in a sewer." This must have been the worse moment of his life. *Can our parents survive exile*? I wonder. *What about my country, my lovely country? Will I ever swim its unspoiled beaches and hike the colorful valleys again? Will I ever breathe the salty air and smell the dampness of its soil following a rainstorm?*

If her family decides to follow, what will Mima do in the US? How will Pipo survive with a law degree from the University of Havana? Cleaning toilets perhaps? Will they end up in Spain or Mexico instead?

Oh my God, will she ever see her family again? And what about Mama and Papa, will he be able to start a business at fifty-five...penniless...and for the hundredth time? And Mama, yes, what about my mother, my disillusioned mother?

I must grow up more in a single night than I had in twenty years.

Following an indisputable victory, Fidel clamps

down even further. As he humiliates and ridicules the northern giant in every speech, Hollywood's Americano image suddenly dissolves in front of our incredulous eyes. So many years of watching American soldiers never lose a battle, so many westerns with Alan Ladd shooting from the hip and eliminating the bad guys, and those WWII movies in which the Americans always won. All those images shattered by an unbearable reality—the loss of freedom...forever. I just can't imagine life without Santa Clauses, Chevy Bel-Airs, conveniences, and tourists. Our powerful neighbor, our beloved Tio Sam, is no more. Poor Cubanos!

The next day is catastrophic at the office. Our mailman had suffered a heart attack the night before, so there are no envelopes to open, no bills to pay, no customer complaints, no invoices, no orders, nothing to distract us from the disaster. Only phone calls from clients, friends, and suppliers opining on the fiasco.

El Chino and Eduardo—the lowest paid workers in the company—agree they'd rather swim across the gulf than work for a communist boss.

"*Ese degenerao cree que to los Cubanos somos estupidos.* That degenerate thinks all Cubans are stupid." says El Chino, referring to Fidel.

"*Pues a mi no me importa lo que el crea, porque aqui en Cuba, no me quedo.* I don't care what he thinks, because I'm not staying in Cuba." Eduardo stands with his hands on his hips. "*Prefiero trabajar pa cualquier patron que pa un comunista come mierda.* I would rather work for any boss than for a communist shithead," he concludes.

We talk and talk all day. Even the old bookkeeper says there is another invasion in the works— "sooner than you may think."

Is Jose hallucinating? I wonder. Is he suffering post-traumatic shock, or has our faithful employee simply lost his mind after the crash?

CHAPTER 17

A Last Trip to Nostalgia

Three weeks following the Bay of Pigs fiasco we traveled by train to the interior of the island to visit my birth town of Camaguey and to introduce Margarita to both sides of the family—nineteen aunts and uncles plus dozens of first and second cousins.

Traditional Camaguey, with its slow pace, was beloved for its colonial architecture, *tinajones* (huge pottery containers), cattlemen wheeling and dealing in the lyceum, horse-drawn carriages or *guarandingas* delivering milk door-to-door at sunrise, bakers swaying their customers to buy their hour-old bread, demijohns filled with mineral water delivered on bicycles, the delightful smell from the town's coffee roaster or *tostadero* scenting the morning mist, the bells of the old cathedral chiming every hour on the hour to remind the faithful to come in and pray, uniformed boys and girls walking to Los Maristas, Los Escolapios, or Las Teresianas for another day of school, and *pregoneros* chanting from their carriages the names of the fruits they are selling:

"*Mangooo, mango manguee de la Torrecillaaa.* Mangos, *mameyes, platanitos manzanos*, papayas, *casera, caserita.*"

And as one strolled along the *callejones,* narrow streets, the pleasing smell of freshly brewed Cuban coffee tells the casual pedestrian that everyone in that house had awakened to another day. Truthfully, nothing could have been more refreshing to the soul than a Camaguey awakening.

But that was the Camaguey of my dreams; the city that once pulsed with life existed no more. All that was left from the sights and sounds of my childhood were feeble echoes and dim images of its glorious past.

The city of Agramonte, the Patriot, the one that saw my entire family come to life, stood still and destitute. In less than two years my beloved Camaguey had ceased to breathe. No more pregones, café cubano, mangos and mameyes, and no more children in uniform. My birthplace stood abandoned and forgotten because the last thing the new class wanted was a connection to the past. Nothing in Cuba was supposed to have a history anymore, much less a glorious one like Camaguey-La Ciudad de los Tinajones.

In the end we were supposed to come from trees, or better yet from a sausage-stuffer—wieners of the same size, flavor, and color, like those produced by Rafael at Embutidos Cubanos, all clones of each other.

Once crowded with devotees awaiting the bells to chime, the entrance to the cathedral stood desolate and its doors half-way open, as if ashamed of what went on inside. Now the bells tolled melancholically and only once a day.

The only people attending mass were the useless, the old, and the pigheaded, for the rest of the faithful were either brainwashed against religion, gone, or afraid that the CDR would eye them as enemies of the new ideology.

The only Supreme Being left in Camaguey, as in the rest of the Alligator Island, was Fidel Castro.

The tropical fruits and veggies sold by pregoneros since time immemorial had mysteriously disappeared from their carts and from dust-covered shelves, and I wondered if the reason for the produce shortage was that, like most animals in a zoo, trees also refused to bear fruit in captivity.

Private and religious schools were nonexistent now, so children attended local indoctrination centers instead. Formerly our number one export, sugar had also vanished from the scene. And what of the town's tostadero with its rich smell of roasted coffee beans? You guessed right; there was no coffee to grind.

After visiting our Camaguey relatives, a reflective experience indeed, we drove to Nuevitas, the backward little town where I spent my early childhood in a house facing a fishing community on one side and a railroad station on the other and where we bought lobsters for *una peseta*, twenty cents, and oysters for a dime a bucket.

Paying a visit to Papa's side of the family wasn't at all pleasant, because my aunt Panchita, a biting spinster who lived with and off my grandparents, had dutifully converted that section of the Rodriguez clan to communism, especially Grandma, whom I had considered an educated and sensible woman until the day she switched to the red team.

Tia Panchita never married, for she refused to *"have any man telling me what to do."* Bragging about her so-called new independence, my aunt embraced the new ideology not because of convictions, but because she resented those having more than she did. Thus, universal poverty became the sedative of choice to choke her chronic envy. Like Grandpa's big-bellied spittoon, plump Tia Panchita was audacious enough to have set up a CDR headquarters at my grandparents' home, and as she got elevated to neighborhood chief spy, the mini-minded bitter woman finally stopped complaining about the unfairness of life.

Credit is due to an uncle of mine for courageously opposing my aunt's venomous intrusions. Following the revolution she never called him brother again, but "the traitor a block away."

"Do you still own the spice business?" Panchita's welcoming words as she opens the door.

"Yes, we do," Margarita snaps back.

"I've heard you two got married in a church." She grins sarcastically.

"Is there any other way?" I say, totally stunned.

"I don't know about you and your wife, but I hate priests with a passion. They're nothing but sanctimonious parasites poisoning the minds of children with a fear of hell, and damn it, they've been at it since the Spanish Inquisition."

Upon our expression of shock she nervously extends her arm to an empty couch in the living room. "But please come in and make yourselves comfortable."

Sitting on a chair across from us, she fretfully clings to its armrests as if ready to detonate.

"Those vultures invented hell to control the minds of their faithful so they could live off them like parasites," Tia continues lecturing. "I'll bet that's the reason the two of you got married in church—fear of hell. Ha! Fear of hell and nothing else!"

Fear of hell my butt! What a welcome! No hello, no glad to see you, no how are you. Not a kind word came from that witch's mouth during our three-day visit. I wished I could punch her cackling mouth right there and then, but I decided to fire back instead.

"How can you say I'm fearful of hell when I've been living in it for two years?"

Margarita pinches my butt to calm me down.

"Besides, Tia, being a communist doesn't give you the right to be so rude," I continue, "and if this is the kind of crap we're going to take while we're here, we might as well leave now."

Out of his study comes Grandpa, the only anti-communist on that side of the family besides my uncle. In clear-cut terms he tells my aunt to apologize and disappear. Unlike Tia Panchita, my grandparents welcome us with open arms.

But there was much more to this relative of mine than just bad manners. Tia Panchita wore fatigues day in and day out. Fatigues she never took off. Not even in bed, for after all, she slept alone. On weekends she volunteered to cut sugar cane from dawn to dusk, adding to the aroma of her fatigues. But what upset neighbors and relatives the most was her self-appointed right to enter any home without knocking in order to snoop on private conversations.

We didn't find as many relatives as I thought in Nuevitas, because most who disagreed with the "perfect state of man" had already left the country, and others who had stayed to enjoy the fruits of the Great Deception deserved, along with Tia Panchita, to live like communists and go to hell as such.

My conversations with Grandpa didn't go far either. As a child I had feared his temper as much as I did Phillips Milk of Magnesia, so we seldom talked. I still remember the day my cousins and I accidentally tore down a rusty chunk of fence chasing a baseball. *Ay Dios mio!* How I wished the earth would've swallowed me right there and then.

All in all what hurt me the most was seeing my grandmother, who used to be so quiet, dedicated, and dignified, brag like a broken record about Cuba's new way of life. Unlike my other set of grandparents, these were dry, stoical, and pragmatic, not spoiling and sweet like Cuban *abuelos* and *abuelas* were supposed to be. Grandma's servitude, despite an impending confiscation of their cattle farm, made my trip to Nuevitas an unforgettable disappointment; therefore I have chosen to believe that her foolish behavior was a result of senility.

At their insistence and because Nuevitas had no decent place to spend the night besides El Gato Negro Hotel, we stayed in the room where Papa was born way back in 1905.

On our last day we visited the little schoolhouse I attended as a youngster by way of a wheelbarrow pushed by one of Papa's trusted helpers. We drove to the beach where I learned to swim at the age of five and to the railroad station from where I took short round-trips to the port of Pastelillo on a nickel's-worth of passage.

"Stay in the train until it comes back to our station, and don't you dare walk on the railroad track, you hear?"

I can still hear Mother's admonition every time I crossed the street to secretly lay a penny ahead of an approaching locomotive. Pennies flattened by the mammoth weight grew large as quarters and thin as paper, pennies that Mama frantically dumped into the trash the day she found out how I got them to look like that.

Following her timely discovery I wasn't allowed to go back and forth to Pastelillo or down to the station anymore.

"Do you want to be flattened by a locomotive? This is the last time you go across the street," Mama yells at me, belt in hand.

I wonder sometimes if the reason I'm writing this today is because of Mama's punishment fifty-some years ago.

CHAPTER 18

The Retreat

The more I saw madness and the longer I gasped for air, the stronger grew my will to leave the insane asylum at any cost.

Our return to Havana was filled with disturbing news: My parents' home had been searched at gunpoint two nights before for "no reason." Nothing incriminating was found, but the police took all passports, including mine. Certainly, the CDR had blown the whistle in our direction.

And Albert Johnson, an American citizen, had left the company and moved to the U.S. because there was no room for an outstanding entrepreneur like him in Castroland anymore. I for one had learned more from that man than in my four years of college. Ethical and fair, A.J. had one of the most brilliant business minds ever to cross my path.

If there was any doubt as to the merit of an escape, those two incidents drove me to dedicate the next few days to finding out the requirements needed to leave Cuba on a plane versus an inner tube.

Valid passports became our first priority; I still had mine to recover, and Margarita had none. We also needed:

- U.S. tourist visas.
- A CDR-certified inventory of all possessions down to the toothbrush, re-certifiable 48 hours prior to the departure of the last household member, assuming he or she would be leaving the country as well.
- An assignment of every piece of property to the government; one missing fork and the entire process had to start all over again.
- Roundtrip tickets bought in US dollars, plus the good fortune of finding empty seats on one of two daily Pan-Am flights Havana-Miami or on the National Airlines flight Kingston-Havana-Miami. Considering the thousands trying to escape, the chances of our getting two empty seats in either one

were dismal.

- A government certificate of exoneration stating that the person leaving the country had no unpaid bills, taxes, or traffic tickets.

Once the above was completed, a last minute body and baggage search at the airport, including optional x-rays, was in order. Baggage allowed: thirty pounds of used clothing, nothing else, and if by chance flights were cancelled because *the Yankees were coming*, or the passenger missed the trip for any reason or someone important wanted his seat, each and every step would have to be repeated over again. By then, of course, the traveling victim had already lost his or her job and was considered a deserter and a pariah in the new society.

Obtaining Margarita's passport and recovering mine was the easiest of the tasks, for Cubans were traveling to the Eastern Bloc, the Soviet Union, and other countries oblivious to our plight, so passports were not necessarily issued only to escapees.

Our next hurdle was to apply for tourist visas, those memorable pieces of paper solicited at the American embassy and issued piecemeal by the U.S. State Department.

Considering that most applicants would wait for a Sunday night or Monday morning to seize their spots at the end of the long line at the American embassy, Margarita and I arrived early on a Friday afternoon, when the file was only three blocks long.

Carrying pillows, camping gear, water bottles, canned foods, raincoats, umbrellas, card games, and so on, we joined the long procession of dissenters waiting to fill out visa applications.

Fortunately we found a nice, shady spot beneath a laurel tree where we could spend the entire weekend eating canned beans, tuna sandwiches, and black-market bananas, and shooting the breeze with an improvised fraternity of Cuban *gusanos*—traitors willing to take abuse from projectile-throwing crowds, unruly fanatics, and passing soldiers shooting at random.

An older lady, her daughter, and three grandchildren stood in front of us. The young woman's husband, in jail for his involvement in the Bay of Pigs fiasco, had begged his wife to leave the country, for she could do much more on his behalf from U.S. soil.

As it turned out, that same young mother became one of the driving forces behind the movement to exchange Bay of Pigs prisoners for farm equipment in 1962.

■ ■ ■

After an entire weekend of sidewalk camping, with sore butts, aching backs, and stiff necks, we awake to Monday morning thundershowers. Thanks to Mima for shoving umbrellas into our *jabucos,* or bags, we don't turn into frogs. At around nine we begin to crawl forward, and by noon we are halfway to the embassy. By then we can't see the end of the line.

"They close at five, you know?" the man behind us says to his wife, who is complaining of pain in her varicose veins.

"The first thing I'll do in Miami is find me *una Americana con dinero* so I don't have to work another day in my life," says a young man in shorts and tennis shoes. "There's no point in breaking my back again, man. All I have is what I'm wearing, and I used to make thousands as a croupier. Now that the rich Americans are gone, I'm following them wherever they are."

"I'm in worse shape than you are, *mi hermano,*" an older guy yells from thirty feet away. "I don't even speak English, and here I am going to the United States. But you know something? I'm *hacha y machete* in dominoes, and that's what Cubans on welfare do in Miami all day. Play dominoes."

"*Mire, compadre, dejeme decirle que en Miami tol'mundo habla español*—everyone in Miami speaks Spanish," shouts another man who seems to know everything about the neighbor from the north and everything about everything. "You should get yourself a job instead of begging for charity. Look at me." He pounds his chest. "I'm planning to work my butt off and make enough money to buy me one of those trailers, a yacht, and go fishing the rest of my life."

What a circus, I think. An entire weekend listening to loud strangers offering unsolicited advice. Braggarts boasting about their former lifestyles, volunteers staging solutions to the personal problems of others, medical troubles brought to light by some hypochondriac in the hope that a certain doctor in the crowd will offer free advice, and if not, perhaps someone who enjoys portraying the role of a physician may offer an oral prescription to treat the malady. And the rumors! Oh, my goodness, the ridiculous good news of Castro suffering from lung cancer and about what will happen to Cuba upon his death; rumors about the Americans forming an army of Cuban exiles to invade the island from Miami. So much hot air helps me realize that, like fish, Cubans' worst enemy isn't Fidel Castro or the despots before him, but our mouths instead.

Finally an embassy employee who must have felt sorry for all of us camping in the rain asks us to split the line in two, for there will be more clerks handling applications.

We get home at around four, and that night nothing could have been more rewarding and soothing to our sore muscles, irritated brains, and stiff necks, than our own wedding present—a brand new Simmons Beautyrest, the last one in stock.

Two weeks later the devil performs another incantation from his Fifth Avenue mansion and the news headlines read like this:

Yankee Imperialists to Recall Their Ambassador Americans Shut Down Embassy

What a blow! The U.S. State Department was canceling all visa applications and offering waivers instead. Such new permits were to be requested directly from Washington, thus making our sixty hours of camping outside the embassy a lost cause.

The most resourceful father in the world, mine, found a second cousin living in Miami who knew someone who worked for the State Department in Washington.

Like John Wayne in *The Fighting Seabees,* Walter came to our rescue, and within three months the waivers arrived. They were only good for a year, so we had to move fast.

The next torment: request an agent from the CDR to take inventory of our belongings.

Oblivious to the risks involved, Margarita concealed her jewels inside a standing marble ashtray in the living room, one day before the search-and-find operation—a reckless act that might have resulted in horrible tragedy. "I just want them back when we return," she said daringly...and we foolishly agreed.

Other than that, nothing else changed inside the house. The same *escobas y trapeadores,* brooms and mops, family movies, albums and portraits, the same superfluous amounts of ladies' shoes, my five-foot-long record collection and underwater fishing gear, Pipo's massive library, Don Luis's hundred-year-old family album, and the sad list went on and on.

Fate had it, though, that Mima would be the one answering for broken glasses and worn toothbrushes at the time of her departure, if it ever came to that, for most considered ludicrous the possibility of America tolerating a communist regime in her own backyard for long. So close...yet so far. Who would have imagined then, that the Alligator Island would be rotting in its own pus for over forty years? And that there would come a time when buying used tennis shoes in Havana would become the luxury of only a few?

The following week, a stout mulatto woman with thick glasses and acute halitosis, and her son, a young man who had forgotten how to smile, are knocking at our door at seven in the morning.

"Welcome raiders! Welcome to Ali Baba's cave," I say to myself. "Help yourselves to anything you want—my record player, Margarita's bedroom set, her cosmetics, wardrobe. Take my underwear and my shoes and my watch. Take everything, but let me get the hell out of here, the sooner the better!"

"Who owns this house?"

Pipo raises a hand, thankfully not his voice.

Knowing we were the ones leaving the country, the woman concentrates her awful-smelling breath on Margarita and me for over two hours of fishing for irrelevant information, such as the amount of sugar stored in the kitchen cabinet, why we lived with her parents instead of on our own, what did we do with the mangoes from the backyard tree, how many times a week did we eat meat, and questions the purpose of which were intended to harass disgruntled citizens already sick and tired of the establishment.

Finally the long-awaited walk begins. The self-appointed civil servant and her son march in front, followed by Mima and the two of us, for thank goodness my fuming father-in-law stays behind.

Probing the marble ashtray, the boy kicks it once...twice...three times. Then he shakes it up and down, complaining that the piece is too heavy for being just that...an ashtray.

My stomach gurgles as I nervously tap my foot on the floor.

"And how much do you expect a marble ashtray to weigh, you fool?" interrupts his mother. "The revolution needs everything inside this house, you hear? Everything! Forget how much things weigh or how good or bad they look. Just count and shut up."

"*Por favor, Mamita,* let me take it apart...*si, o no?*"

"*Callate, coño!*"

Disregarding her angry remark, the restless boy persists. "*Anda, anda,* let me open it! It shouldn't take more than a minute...."

"I've told you never to question my judgment in front of others, haven't I?"

"Yes, Mamita, but this is different. I know it is."

"Another word from that big mouth of yours and I'll send you back to your father for a beating, so shut up and count."

The frightening match hopefully over, we walk into the library where Grandpa, as always, is reading the paper.

"You're too old to leave, man; you're too damn old," the boy snaps at Don Luis. He pulls Pipo's pricey set of binoculars from their leather case and looks at them in idiotic wonderment while Big Mama scrutinizes everything slowly and patiently, one small, excruciating step at a time, for as they say—the devil is in the details.

Caressing a Lalique vase atop the bookcase, she slowly flips the pages of almost every book to ensure that nothing of value is buried in between.

"Remind me to count those National Geographic magazines before we leave," she orders her son.

Marching into Mima's bedroom she heads for the closet, the armoire, and every piece of furniture with drawers and doors.

Tossing the contents of tightly organized drawers atop the bed and on the floor, Spy Jr. excavates for that one-of-a-kind scoop that will catapult him up to the next level of undercover agents.

"Shake'm up and make sure there's nothing inside but clothing," Mama tells little Sherlock Holmes, who nods grudgingly.

Slapping in front of her some of Mima's most expensive dresses, the woman swirls her hippo-hips in front of a mirror. "You definitely have expensive taste, woman," she says, writing the official count on government paper and her personal comments on a flat grocery bag as a crude reminder of which garments fit her best.

Finally, we move into our bedroom.

"Who's the one with the tacky taste around here?" she asks facetiously. "Why would anyone decorate a bedroom so *concentrically*?"

"Y a usted que le importa? That's none of your business," Mima replies, beside herself.

"It is certainly my business, lady," the woman replies furiously, pointing here and there. "I'm the law here, I'm the law there, and I'm the law everywhere, you understand?" Mima glowers at her.

"I said, do you understand? Answer me!"

"Yes, of course I understand, Mima says," her eyes alight as if possessed.

Following the humiliating encounter, the woman inspector tames herself somewhat, for she knows that Margarita's family still has friends in high places, and by rocking the boat she could be chancing the opportunity to grab some of the goodies already set aside on the grocery bag list.

It takes two solid days for the queen of halitosis and her spawn to finish the count, and after all is said and done she leaves without a goodbye or a thank you.

That night I share three Bacardi mojitos with my father-in-law, Mima takes Meprobamato to be able to sleep, and Margarita desperately stuffs the ashtray with lots and lots of toilet paper to secure its contents.

"Did you notice the boy eyeing my TV set every time he passed by it?" says Don Luis.

"You haven't seen anything yet," replies my father-in-law. "Let's hope nothing is missing or broken when the last person leaves the house."

CHAPTER 19

The Long Wait

The six longest months of my life had passed by without a peep from Pan-Am. Meanwhile, Castro was considering compulsive military duty for all men under twenty-two.

My visa waiver would expire in four months, and if the draft was adopted I would be required to join the militia for two years. Me? Fight for Fidel Castro? What a joke! Worst scenario: I'd be getting us a couple of inner tubes to cross the gulf.

For some reason the certificate of exoneration was the most difficult document to obtain, so while we waited for the airline tickets, Mima asked her brother-in-law Alberto—the doctor who had joined Fidel in the mountains—to use his influence in getting the darn paper signed and released by the government. While hundreds of thousands waited anxiously for the certificates, we got them via courier the following day.

Idealists at heart, Alberto and his wife Daisy were no fools. Four years following their triumphant procession into the capital, the couple flew on a government mission to Madrid, where they asked the US embassy for political asylum. Validating his degree from the University of Havana, Alberto eventually became a prominent Florida anesthesiologist.

We were set to go except for the airline tickets. Oh, my God, those darn lottery tickets! I couldn't sleep, eat, or think straight considering that any day Margarita and I would be arriving in Miami...free at last.

I felt so remorseful watching Margarita preparing to abandon all things dear and meaningful to her. Torn at the seams, she was eagerly uprooting herself from everyone and everything she loved, to resurrect in a foreign land for our sake and that of our descendants.

Ache after ache, we began to realize that achieving and enjoying freedom was not a birthright. No, it wasn't. And it wasn't cheap either...it never had been and never will be. Our only hope was that America would welcome us into its Land of Opportunity.

Of course, we realized beforehand that it would be entirely up to us to share in our new society and pay for such privilege in installments, one experience at a time.

On the other hand, we never anticipated the ordeals facing refugees entering a foreign country with no money, no language, no idea of its idiosyncrasies, laws, and customs, the shenanigans of finding a job—what kind and where? Had I ever considered making a living on a dollar an hour? Who would have imagined that Blue Cross Blue Shield weren't affiliates of the Knights of Columbus? Why in God's name we would need a social security number when there was nothing social or secure about it? And what the hell was income tax?

■ ■ ■

"Here they are, Andy, *se acabaron tus penas,* your tribulations are over. I'll bet the tickets are inside." First to bring in the mail, Don Luis wittily flips a yellow wrapper in front of me. Smelling like brand new money, our magic carpet to the free world lies inside the manila envelope.

Twenty-four hours before departure, a telegram with the flight date and seat assignments is supposed to arrive. Nervous tension sets in.

CHAPTER 20

Adios, Alligator Island

Aggravation number one: my telegram arrived that week; Margarita's didn't, so she wasn't leaving. Would she leave next week, next month, next year? Would she ever leave? Was I right to depart alone? Soon our enthusiasm dissolved into frustration and worry. I felt like a baffled stone crab, for every step we took forward we took two backwards.

"You must go, Andy. She'll leave after you, even if it takes going back to Alberto for another favor." Mima's words were encouraging, but

167

still...Margarita wasn't coming.

I drove to my parents' to say goodbye. They were also waiting for airline tickets and for the vet's certificate of health to take Crispin, the dog, out of the country.

Margarita didn't drive in those days and Pipo was out of town, so I called Enrique for a ride to the airport the next morning.

During that sleepless night I amused myself prying the rubber layer off my shoe heel to insert an American dime in-between. Enough for one phone call to Mr. Johnson upon arrival in Miami. That was all I would need...I thought.

September 30, 1961. My duffle bag is jam-packed, and Enrique is knocking at the door at eight in the morning. The plane leaves at one. It's time to go.

"Call Mr. Johnson when you land in Miami," I say to Margarita. "He'll tell you where I am."

Amazingly enough there are no tears. Hesitation and anxiety must have taken them away. Mima feigns enthusiasm. "What God has in mind for you, Andy, will come regardless; have faith and the sky will clear."

"Come on, man, it's time to go!" Enrique drags the duffle bag with one hand and pulls my arm with the other. "You'll see her in no time—come on!"

Margarita jolts me with a hug so powerful it

feels as if we're imploding unto each other. I never knew she had so much strength.

With a racing heart, a twisted stomach, and a splitting headache, I get inside the car.

Enrique drops me at the main entrance. In the concourse there's a large seating area with glass all around known as the fishbowl—*la pescera.* Relatives and friends would stay out watching the lucky passengers inside, awaiting the physical search and further harassment, aimed generally at men. Don't ask me why, but women were rarely bothered.

After offering my seat to a lady, I sit atop the duffle bag for about two hours. It actually takes that long for me to realize that they are calling passengers in alphabetical order, so the R's will be among the last ones going in.

There are children in the fishbowl, some nervous, some cranky, others asleep. Most are traveling with friends or relatives...or are being sent alone to orphanages by desperate parents. There is also a family of five Rodriguezes traveling together. *What a lucky bunch*, I think. *They must know someone higher up than Alberto.*

Conversation is loud and unremitting, just like at the American embassy—free advice, free medical consultation, but no freedom to say what we really want to...not yet.

"Rodriguez! *El senor Fernando Rodriguez, si-*

game. Y quitese el saco; que estamos en Cuba y aqui no hay frio," the woman in fatigues says to Fernando Rodriguez. "Take off your winter coat and follow me. Don't forget you're still in Cuba."

"My name starts with an A and his with an F. Why haven't they called me?" I mutter.

"Hijo, no se ponga nervioso que ahorita le toca a usted. Acuerdese que esta noche va a dormir en Miami," says the older lady to whom I had offered my seat and whose surname begins with a Y. "Son, don't get nervous for I'm sure you'll be next. Just remember, you're sleeping in Miami tonight."

"Andres Rodriguez..."

"Hey, ese soy yo! That's me; that's me."

"Sigame hasta la oficina del camarada Antonio y no grite tanto!" Shut up and follow me to Comrade Antonio's office." The woman in fatigues ushers me to one of the cubicles.

Past the fishbowl and toward the gate, private closet-sized rooms remind me of a doctor's office. Each has a small desk and two chairs, one for an armed soldier and a smaller one across his desk for the runaway victim to sit, relax, and enjoy more maddening questions. A rectangular bench used for duffle bag inspections stands alongside the wall, and behind the soldier's chair a smaller door with a top window leads to the tarmac and the DC6.

Without the courtesy of a greeting I'm told to sit

across from this icon with long hair and a face full of zits. Stroking a long beard that reaches to the center of his chest, the twenty-some-year-old soldier in black beret and camouflage uniform has so much grime under his nails that they crudely resemble those of an ape.

The henchman pulls a thick folder from a file cabinet and opens it in front of me. A form with my name on it appears on top of the pile.

"Is this you?" he asks with virtually pursed lips.

"Yes, sir, that's me," I say, shaking on my seat.

"Stand up and take your clothes off."

As I'm undressing, the Pan Am plane shines through the window. What a terrific sight! It's even more exciting than Viñales.

"I didn't say to take off your shorts, you idiot. Machos don't touch other men's parts, didn't you know that?"

As I'm pulling them back up, Antonio grabs my wallet.

"Mmm. *Bonita hembra, eh? Es tu mujer?* Nice looking broad, is she your wife?"

"Yes...she is."

He hurls the billfold atop the table and looks inside every compartment to ensure nothing's missing. Unhappy with "no findings" he digs further and further with a pocket knife.

"Mmm, I can't believe my eyes," he yells, tossing the wallet irately on the floor. "Bad news, Rodriguez, I have very, very bad news for you: you are not going anywhere. Put on your clothes and sit down; you're under arrest."

The stoolie from hell with his pocket knife has found an unpaid parking ticket, accidentally crushed inside my wallet.

The situation is desperate, for I have also forgotten to unclip Margarita's engagement present, a gold Parker pen, from my shirt pocket before leaving home. I'm tempted to throw it in the trash can nearby, but it's already too late because Comrade Antonio has his greedy eyes fixed on it. *Damn it!* I think. H*ow can I be so thick? Now they'll throw me in jail for smuggling gold out of the country.*

All of a sudden Mima's words resound in the hollow cavity of my foolish head: "What God has waiting for you, Andy, will come regardless."

Right there and then my guardian angel douses enough adrenaline on me to take charge of the situation. If I'm going to rot in jail for smuggling gold, I might as well bribe the bastard and go for broke.

"Companero Antonio; my not paying the fine was an involuntary transgression against the Department of Transit, and I'm extremely sorry for carrying out such a despicable act against the revolution. On the other hand, comrade, may I implore you to take this gold pen to Transit at your convenience and offer it in full atonement of my offense? This, Comrade Antonio, is only between you and me and no one else, as I'm sure you'll agree this is a fair and honorable way of atoning for my stupid mistake."

Yanking the gold pen from my pocket, Antonio caresses it cautiously and with suspicion. He turns around to make certain no one's looking through the rear window, opens the office door, and snaps it shut after ensuring the hall is deserted. Thank God, no one has been listening. Narrowing his contemptuous eyes, the visibly pleased bully seizes me by the hair and produces a revolver, the barrel of which he presses firmly against my neck.

The incorruptible patriot whispers menacingly in my ear.

"Listen, you s.o.b, I'm not even going to check your duffle bag or your shoes. It's too late to play games. Pick up the sack and walk straight to the plane with your head down. If I see you talking to anyone before boarding, and I don't give a damn if it's Fidel himself, I'll put a bullet in your brain. Then I'll drag your body to the morgue as a traitor attempting to bribe a soldier of the revolution. You get that, my boy?" The comrade cagily hides my pen inside his briefcase.

"Yyyessir, I do."

"I'm sure you do. Now take your bag full of shit

and go!"

Every step of the way I feel he is going to shoot me. Antonio probably didn't only because he was smart enough to conceal his gutless machismo before the American flight crew.

A half-hour following my encounter with the loyal flag-waver, the plane cranks its engines on. I can't wait to see my poisoned soil from above the clouds.

At ten past one we are flying above the beaches of Santa Maria del Mar north of Havana, where Margarita and I went picnicking so many times. In the distance, I also make out the small town of Cojimar—the fishing village that inspired Ernest Hemingway to write his Nobel Prize- winning novel *The Old Man and the Sea.*

Will I ever see my wife again? What about my beloved Alligator Island? I wonder in dismay.

With a stomachache and a heart running wild, I call the flight attendant.

"Miss, I need to use your restroom. Can I please go now?"

"You don't have to ask, sir. Here, would you like some gum?"

With my deepest appreciation to the Parker Pen Company: *Viva la libertad!*

CHAPTER 21

Welcome To Miami

Bienvenidos a Miami signs hang every-where along the concourse. Children waving Cuban and American flags from the shoulders of those awaiting passengers paint the perfect image of an indoor parade. On the opposite side of the retaining cord, a middle-aged woman trying to reach her inbound husband is so energized by his arrival that she shouts his name over and over at the top of her voice. Laughter and tears blend into the confusion, and in the midst of it I'm stunned by the fact that I have become a free man in less than fifty-five minutes. As eerie as it sounds, I feel as though I have resurrected from the dead. Moreover, in spite of the heat and the sweating at Havana's airport, I still carry a hint of Margarita's hair lotion on my shirt and the oppression of her absence in my heart.

Waving a sign with my name on it, Albert Johnson is trying to make his way up front.

"You'll be taken to a detention camp in Opa-Locka for two or three days," says my Cuban-American friend, shaking hands above the crowd. "Don't worry, they won't send you back. Call me upon your release to pick you up."

A Spanish-speaking immigration officer approaches the arriving passengers.

"Women, children, men over sixty, those traveling with their families, and everyone entering the country with regular visas, follow the signs to Immigration and Customs. The rest, please follow me."

About twenty of us are led to an empty room somewhere in the airport's lower level.

"From here you'll be taken along with your duffle bags to a military camp. You'll be debriefed for a half hour every morning," the officer tells us. "Once in the camp you'll be able to phone anyone, anywhere in the world. Accommodations are far from the Hilton, but adequate. There will be books, movies, card games, and so on to make yours a relaxed and happy stay. A word of warning though:

Do not attempt to leave the premises. Understood?"

A chorus of yeses follows.

"Are there any questions or concerns?"

"Why are we being interrogated? Does the government think we're spies?" asks a young man about my age.

"First, please understand that you come from a communist country. Second, the State Department has waived your visa rights and is using a loophole in the law to enable you to enter the US, so theoretically your stay won't become legal until certain procedures are followed, and I hate to say it, sir, but this is one of them."

"How can we call home without money?" asks someone whose family was left behind.

"You won't need any as long as you're at the camp. Phone calls are free, and we'll give you fifty dollars upon release.

"Gentlemen, welcome to the United States."

At camp we are assigned a Puerto Rican officer who obviously wants to turn us into soldiers. At five in the morning Sargento Gonzalez blows his whistle to take us for a run around the track. An hour later he leads us to the showers, and in exactly ten minutes he has us marching into the mess hall for breakfast. At ten he takes us to our briefing officers for an hour of questioning. At noon we have lunch, followed by a two-hour break or a full siesta for those out of shape. Calisthenics before dinner plus another shower, and by eight sharp we must climb into our bunks and go to sleep at the sound of Sargento Gonzales's maddening toot.

Everyone takes the experience lightheartedly and without complaints. The fact we are finally in a free country and that the questioning is mostly symbolic makes our stay at the camp uniquely satisfying. My only concern, especially at bedtime, is the distressing thought of a lovely wife left behind.

According to Margarita, on the same day as my departure, a CDR delegate stopped by our house to disclose some irregularities in the inventory, meaning she'd have to start the ridiculous procedure all over again unless the Department of the Interior formally accepted the count as filed.

The next morning Mima called Alberto for help, and before the day was over the required statement of acceptance arrived via courier, along with a telegram assigning Margarita a seat on the same flight the next day.

Although unaware of new developments back home, I dwelled constantly on my wife's heartbreaking agony at leaving her loved ones behind, especially Grandpa, whom she might never see again. Although her early departure surprised me, I realized once again that nothing in human society can be more valuable than friends and relatives in high places.

Following an emotionally charged farewell, Margarita left Jose Marti Airport en route to Miami, where Mr. Johnson, at Papa's request, waited to take her to his home in Key Biscayne.

While the majority of Cuban émigrés of the early sixties belonged to the deposed upper and middle class—educated individuals with business skills, financial resources, ambition, energy, and a willingness to start from scratch—there were others with no education or means just as desperate to leave the Alligator Island.

In spite of their disadvantages many of these underprivileged refugees eventually became much more productive in American society than they were in Cuba when they left. Yet, others with stronger resources and more brainpower never amounted to a head of cabbage. In the new scenario, survival skills were often more essential than money and education.

Once in Miami, confused, alone, and distressed, Margarita followed Mr. Johnson to baggage claim, where someone tapped her shoulder as she was fetching her duffle bag. To her enormous surprise it was my cousin Pedrito and his pregnant wife Maria, who had come to welcome an uncle of hers who never arrived.

My cousin told Margarita he had left Cuba almost a year before, when the U.S. embassy was still in business. He'd gotten married in Miami and at the moment was working for Eastern Airlines as an apprentice mechanic at $1.75/hr.

The unexpected couple gave Margarita their phone number and address in Hialeah with the promise that we would see each other after my release. Needless to say, the encounter made my wife feel much more at ease.

She was then taken to Key Biscayne. But it happened that the Johnsons were expecting a large group of family to arrive by week's end. Margarita had to find another place to stay in less than seventy-two hours.

The following morning Mrs. Johnson took her to the Cuban Refugee Center in Miami to request my release from camp and to finish some paperwork.

That afternoon an Opa-Locka school bus carrying twenty Cuban immigrants, including myself, arrived at the Center for Refugee Affairs in Miami to receive the fifty-dollar bill and to ratify our "free on parole" status—the legal loophole that allowed us to stay until we attained permanent residence standing later on. At that moment I yanked the dime from my heel to call the Johnsons.

Although I can't truthfully evoke my reaction at hearing the sound of Margarita's voice, it must have been at least startling enough for one of the center volunteers to ask if I was okay.

CHAPTER 22

El Exilio

Early the following morning Maria showed up at the Johnsons' home unexpectedly. She had come to take us back to the refugee center to apply for financial assistance-one hundred dollars a month until we were able to survive on our own. In addition to the first check, they would also give us a five-pound can of dehydrated eggs, five pounds of powdered milk, a large package of corn meal, and ten cans of Spam—a generous deed from our newly adopted country to ensure all Cuban refugees survived to tell the tale.

"Pedrito and I want you two to stay in our empty bedroom until you have a place of your own. It's the most sensible thing to do and we won't take no for an answer," Maria said, pulling out of the driveway.

Given that our other options were a half-way house or a public shelter, we accepted their offer with sincere gratitude.

Their apartment was tiny: a living room-dinette, a small kitchen, two baths, and two bedrooms, one of which only had a bare mattress on the floor. Even though he had been in Miami for about a year, it wasn't until recently, and precisely when Maria's belly began to grow, that Pedrito landed his buck-seventy-five-an-hour job at Eastern, and they still had to buy all the etceteras needed to accommodate the coming baby.

In those needy days I only spoke a little English and Margarita knew some basic grammar she had learned from a private tutor in Havana. Speaking the language almost fluently, Maria took upon herself the mission of orientation. She worked part-time in a doctor's office as a receptionist, and on her next morning off she drove us through town in their carefully maintained vintage Ford, coaching us on how to save money on groceries. We visited several supermarkets so we could learn the English names of certain things and the American way of buying groceries.

She also showed us the quirks of Miami's traffic and the different routes of public transportation. To educate us in the art of shopping, she took us to Burdines, Richards, and Jackson Byrons—the city's largest department stores in those days. Can you imagine anyone in this country with a shopping disability?

"In Miami," Maria said, "the stop sign is what determines the right of way. Remember, only the stop sign...nothing else. Blowing the horn like in Cuba will get you in trouble fast; in fact, no one here uses it except to avoid an accident. And do you see that sign that reads US 95? It doesn't mean you can drive at ninety-five miles an hour. It just tells you the number of the highway. And to take a left, don't wait for simultaneous yellow and green lights like in Havana; just turn left on green faster than the approaching car."

"That sounds dangerous!" Margarita exclaimed.

"Oh, you'll get used to it. And something very important: After a bed, the first thing you'll need to buy is a car; that is, if you don't want to spend an entire day sweating, waiting for a bus. I also suggest you learn to drive, Margarita, the sooner the better."

For three consecutive nights we all went to sleep past midnight, because these good Samaritans dedicated their little quality time to sitting around the table and explaining the system's do's and don't's, such as the need to buy health insurance, the reasons for getting a social security number, the moral responsibility of becoming US citizens later in life, and finally the longest and most complicated of all lessons: the concept of income tax. Thanks to their selfless dedication we were able to crawl in the right direction when we didn't even know which way was up.

During our four-day stay we shared the cost of food, for it wasn't fair to add an extra ounce to their financial load. Besides, despite their honest desire to lend a hand, I always felt we were imposing. So upon our insistence Maria took us all over town to look for places that were in good condition, close to bus stops, safe...and cheap, for in the end, we had only a hundred dollars left.

After a fruitless day of calling and driving the classifieds, we accidentally stopped in front of an apartment complex in which most tenants were either walking on crutches or driving wheelchairs. It was the kind of place one would identify today as an assisted living community. We certainly knew there were some 200,000 Cuban refugees in Miami, many of them looking for jobs, but we were less aware of the enormous number of senior citizens coming into the area.

"Let's get off right here," said Maria.

"Allenda Apartments?"

"Someone's name, I guess. Let's talk to the manager and see what we can do. I have a gut feeling this is going to work."

As it happened, their only vacancy was a 350-square-foot efficiency long vacated by an elderly woman who had committed suicide as a result of senile dementia. The place came with sofa bed, stove, and most of the essentials to make it livable, except for good air conditioning and a shower. The plumbing in the small bathroom clattered through the night and hardly worked during the day.

"No one wants to rent this place because they think it's jinxed," said the manager, an elderly woman who spoke with a German accent and moved with a walker.

"Even the old man who lived here prior to this lady passed away of unknown causes," the obese lady continued. "Our community is very superstitious when it comes to dying. I'm sure you can appreciate that...even at your age."

"Hmm. This woman is either too honest, or she's looking for an excuse to rent it to someone else," Maria whispered in Spanish.

"How much do you want?"

"A hundred-twenty a month, plus a hundred-dollar deposit," said the manager.

After lots of haggling and begging, Maria finally cut a deal with the woman: First month

$80.00, second month $100.00, and $120.00 there-after. No deposit. The bottom line: we had $20.00 left for an entire month. Not too shabby.

On Sunday morning Pedrito and Maria moved us to our first home in the United States, the number two apartment at the Allenda Assisted Living Community complex.

In those days, Mr. Johnson and a couple of Cuban partners had purchased a small meat-packing plant right across the street from the airport, and they were trying to make a go of it with their backs against the wall. It was tough for three immigrants to penetrate the American market when two of them didn't speak English.

Monday morning I called him at the plant.

"Do you think there's a chance I can work for you guys?"

"Of course there is, but we can't afford to pay more than sixty cents an hour, and the only opening we have now is with the cleaning crew at night. If you don't mind the hours and the pay, come see me tomorrow morning."

Gee, that's only five bucks a night, I thought in dismay. "That's okay, I'll take it!"

After an early morning breakfast of eggs scrambled in hot water and slices of Spam breaded in corn flour and fried by someone who had never cooked, Margarita packed me a leftover lunch with a catsup sandwich; for catsup, according to Maria, was an excellent source of food variety. I went to see Mr. Johnson while Margarita stayed home to practice her English.

Due to our massive immigration, a rift between the Cuban community and African Americans grew wider by the day. Hungrier and better educated, most of us would work for equal or less pay and produce better quality work, more efficiently, and in a shorter period of time. Understandably, many detested us for taking their jobs, and it so happened that since one of the Norge Packing Co. Cuban employees had been arrested and imprisoned for assaulting a black worker the day before, I was immediately hired as a part-time substitute, in addition to the night crew.

That day, my task consisted of stacking hundreds of twenty-pound ground beef boxes inside the freezer, a job I began at eight and finished by noon. At one o'clock I was moving the same pallets into a refrigerated truck, and by six I was all done. The assignment used to take two men the same amount of time; no wonder by the end of the day my arms were numb and my right hand nearly frostbitten, due to missing fingers in one of the thermal gloves.

My dinner menu that evening included five slices of Polish sausage chased by two cups of café cubano so I could stay up for the night shift. Since we didn't have a phone, I called Margarita at the Allenda manager's office.

"I'm going nuts with this darn English, and I'm not feeling well," she complained.

"What's the matter, are you ill?"

"I think that powdered milk is making me sick to my stomach. Just looking at it makes me feel nauseous."

"Oh, my God, you're not pregnant, are you?"

"I don't think so. How about you? Are you okay?"

"I'm fine except for my three fingers."

"When are you coming home?"

"Tomorrow morning."

"Tomorrow morning? You must be kidding!"

"No, I'm not. I need to work fourteen hours straight to bring home some money."

There was silence at the other end of the line. Margarita didn't like it, but she understood.

"Just do me a favor," she said with a sigh. Please stay out of the freezer, okay? All we need now is for you to catch pneumonia or lose a finger."

That night I met my gregarious steam-cleaning partner, Eladio, a former law professor from a private university in Havana, now nicknamed El Doctor by fellow employees. He showed me how to sterilize the equipment, the floors, the walls, and the roof. It seemed as though he thoroughly enjoyed that sort of work; but then he said that the State Meat Inspector was some kind of bigot who liked to harass Cubans and blacks, so he wanted to ensure that everything was cleaned to the point of sterility before the guy came in the next morning.

"I just want to show el *come mierda ese* (sucker) that Cubans can do things equally well or better than anyone else."

Eladio and I worked almost till dawn, my first fourteen hour shift...a depressing revelation that money, unlike mangoes, doesn't grow on trees. At exactly four, El Doctor, who by then had had over twenty *cafecitos,* offered me a ride home because *en Miami todo esta cerca*—in Miami everything is close by. Since every employee was allowed to take home a pound of finished product, I grabbed two packages of fresh pork sausage for breakfast.

Driving like a maniac at four-thirty in the morning, caffeine-laden Eladio must have broken every traffic rule laid down by Maria. The man had to be at another job at eight sharp, and he wanted to see his two daughters before they left for school.

"Do you sleep at all?"

"Only four hours, Andy. Don't forget, I have a wife and two kids."

Once at the apartment I went straight to kiss my wife good morning. Being around sausages for so long, awakening her was like embracing a bush blooming with gardenias.

After a breakfast of fried pork sausage and corn fritters dipped in catsup, I went to bed. Sweet dreams, Andy; today you're sleeping with a full stomach and twenty dollars in Margarita's purse.

By noon I was on my way back to the sausage factory for six hours of substitution and another night of steam-cleaning.

Also as of that day, Maria would be picking up Margarita every afternoon to help her find a job—a difficult task indeed, given that Miami's Cuban community was still small and the need for Spanish-speaking help was virtually nonexistent.

Since Maria's uncle and my parents were due to arrive any time, the two always checked the Pan Am list of passengers scheduled to land the next day, and it so happened that on one of those trips to the airport, Margarita bumped into Dolores, the mother of Nancy, a former friend from school.

"*Hija, por el amor de Dios,* child, for the love of God, what in the world you are doing here all by yourself?" she asked. "You look so pale and under-nourished. Where's your husband? Oh, you look so awful. Are you eating well? Are you pregnant?"

Introducing herself, Maria told Dolores not to worry, for she and Pedrito had also gone through the same ordeal and survived. So daunted was Nancy's mother by Margarita's famished look that the next day she showed up at our apartment with a pot full of *arroz con pollo,* and if that wasn't enough she kept bringing us food twice a week for an entire month, "to make sure we didn't catch scurvy as a result of malnutrition." Each time, Dolores stayed long enough to show Margarita how to cook Cuban recipes. Her husband, Roberto, had left Cuba early enough to transfer ten thousand dollars to an American bank, so in contrast to most, they were considered wealthy refugees.

Two weeks into my part-time work at the meat mixer, the feisty Cuban was released from jail, reclaimed his former job, and mine was reduced to the night shift at sixty cents an hour. After saving one hundred dollars and losing twenty pounds in the process, we invited Pedrito and Maria for dinner at the Royal Castle—a pre-Burger King chain in Miami.

"I may be stuck with $1.75 hr. for a while, but after the baby is born and the sky clears, I'm doing something different for a living," said my cousin, adding catsup to his French fries. "And if I were you, Andy, I'd quit that sixty-cent slave deal and find a better job or a way to work for yourself, even if it's cleaning windows or mowing lawns."

Pedrito's words echoed in my head all night long. He was absolutely right.

Incredible enough my cousin and I became very close friends. Nothing in this world brings more harmony among people than the mutual sharing of misery...feisty relatives included.

That Friday, Maria took us to the airport to welcome my parents and Crispin the dog, who decided to pee all over the baggage claim area after leaving the kennel.

Free at last, Father was ecstatic. I hadn't seen my old man so ebullient in years. Mama, on the other hand, was in a bath of tears.

"I don't know why I cry," she said, all confused. "I just can't control myself."

With a couple of thousand dollars from an insurance policy deposited in an American bank long before Batista, they were able to afford a modest hotel for the time being. But because of the excitement, the talking, and the way Cubanos are, we forgot to exchange whereabouts.

CHAPTER 23

The Trip Downtown

Thoroughly embarrassed, Margarita embarked on a guilty mop-up mission the following day: Call every downtown hotel asking for guests registered under the name Rodriguez. A long day of inquiries produced no leads, so the next morning she headed back to the city center, searching for a Cuban family with a black and white dog named Crispin.

After wandering for hours, she called me at work.

"There must be a better way to do this. My feet

hurt, it's too hot outside, and I still feel nauseous, so I'm going home."

"Why don't you buy a gallon of real milk on your way over and throw away that hideous stuff? Enough is enough! Also, instead of finding my parents this way, let's wait for Mr. Johnson to come back from his trip. I'm sure he knows where they are."

At home that evening, Margarita told me about a girl she had met on the bus coming back. Her name was Gabriella.

"Please call me Gaby; everyone knows me by that name."

In their exchange Gaby tipped off Margarita to an opening at the Jackson Byrons department store where she worked.

"But how can I sell anything without speaking the language?"

"Listen; all you have to do is drop by tomorrow morning right after ten and ask for me. I'll introduce you to the manager, and all you have to say is yes or no, depending on my signal. Just come over and we'll see what happens. It's worth a shot, Margarita. Anyway, the manager likes me and he's a nice guy."

Outgoing, thin as air, and dressed too smartly for a Cuban exile, Gaby's contagious smile radiated an enthusiasm rarely seen among struggling refugees. Her boundless energy toward adversity gave this remarkable gal a personality impossible to dislike and her delicate manners an air difficult to overlook.

According to Margarita, this is what took place at the Jackson Byron store Tuesday morning at ten.

"Mr. Bailey, this is my step-sister, Margarita—you know, like the white and yellow flower? She's also from Havana, and speaks a little English—I'd say good enough to become the same top salesperson she was at her uncle's clothing store in Havana. She's also like me, Mr. Bailey; organized, customer-oriented, honest, and above all, sir, she'll never miss a day of work unless she's run over by a car or gets pregnant. You understand?"

"Are you married, Margarita?" asks Mr. Bailey.

Gaby nods in agreement.

"Husband works sausage company," says Margarita.

Pressing the index finger against her lips, Gaby shakes her head slightly.

"Where do you live, young lady?"

"She lives by my house, Mr. Bailey, so we can even come to work together."

"What's your last name?"

Margarita understands this question from her studies.

"Minsal, sir."

"I'm sorry, Mr. Bailey, but she just came from

Cuba where wives don't adopt their husband's sur-names," chimes in Gaby. "Here in Miami she would be Margarita Rodriguez. That's Rodriguez with a *g*, for she's Cuban, not Mexican."

"We'll be paying you a dollar an hour every day from one to four, including Sundays. Does it sound reasonable?"

Gaby nods acquiescently. Margarita follows, smiling her most charming smile.

A few more questions arise until the generous store manager pulls a job application from his file cabinet and hands it to Gaby.

"Make sure your step-sister fills out every line and signs it at the bottom." Barely concealing a grin, Mr. Bailey stands up and leaves the room.

Exceptionally kind, Mr. Bailey was the kind of person who could easily fall prey to the needs and desires of others. In his early sixties, unsightly as Lincoln and rather shy, the gracious boss thoroughly enjoyed the adulation of younger females, with whom he joked all the time. How he held his position for almost thirty years without being seriously victimized by scoundrels was, according to Gaby, an act of Divine Providence.

Coached by her new friend and encouraged by their boss, Margarita was made responsible for stocking, inventorying, classifying, and pricing garments, for she didn't have the verbal skills to deal with the public, a handicap Mr. Bailey knew from the beginning. To help her learn the language, all instructions were given in English, and Gaby virtually refused to speak Spanish in her presence.

The first day at work an older clerk asked Margarita to help her fold and classify some garments on the shelf.

"Honey, will you please hand me the Polo shirts on that table so I can fold them inside those drawers?"

Palo shirts? Margarita wondered at her first_as-signment. *What does she means by palo? I don't see any_stick around here. Why would she ask me for a piece of wood? Palo shirts, palo shirts? Dios Mio, what in the world is she talking about?*

"No, no, no, dear; not the broom. I'm talking about the Polo shirts—p-o-l-o. You know what Polo shirts are? Here, I'll show you."

For some reason this funny incident has lived in my wife's mind ever since. Did I say funny? Mmm. I guess I did. Not in those days, though.

The family eventually got together upon Mr. Johnson's return, and within two weeks we were all moving into a three-bedroom house four blocks east of a marginal neighborhood called Allapattah and five blocks from Jackson Byrons.

Embedded in the sixty-year-old house was that peculiar odor of mold so evident inside Florida homes without air conditioning, more so when the same carpet had been in use for over twenty years.

In its tiny backyard grew the largest avocado tree in creation, with fruits almost as big as footballs.

I always wondered what would happen if one of those pulpy green bombs ever fell on someone's head from the tallest branch. I for one avoided its shade during avocado season.

The dwelling also came with a garage full of junk, courtesy of its owner, Mr. Bolton, and the monthly rent for the essentially furnished house was $150.00. This, equally shared among two families, enabled us to stash about fifty dollars every month.

Selling Mr. Johnson's hams and sausages to restaurants, delis, and institutions, Father also began to make a little money. Storing them in an ice box inside the trunk of his 1949 Oldsmobile, Papa would drive hundreds of miles and knock on door after door for a few dimes-worth of profit.

Without a doubt these were tough times for people over fifty to make a living, and Papa had struggled throughout his life to afford us a better livelihood. Then, bang! Fidel confiscated everything he owned and worked so hard for, in exchange for permission to leave the country. But the man who passionately loathed communism valued freedom highly enough to make it worthy of the sacrifice. Persistence in the face of adversity was his forte and surviving exile his ultimate challenge.

Now, before I get too sidetracked on another topic, let's go back to the garage full of junk and the old yard equipment—including Mr.Bolton's lawnmower. The engine sounded and smoked like a locomotive, the cord had to be pulled dozens of times to get it to start, and the cutting blade, seemingly made of balsa wood, wouldn't hurt a stalk of grass unless it ran over it three or four times. But it so happened that upon rebuilding the prehistoric machine, I began to consider mowing area lawns for two dollars a shot. Ten lawns on Saturdays and ten on Sundays would bring me forty dollars in only two days of work.

The first Saturday, I offered my services to not less than twenty homes whose lawns grew up to my ankles, but since just a few owners were willing to pay the price, I only mowed three. On Sunday I mowed four, and one of them had so much dog poop on it that I decided to quit half-way into the job, never to return.

It took me several weeks to gather ten steady customers, and for those, one paid me with bouncing checks half the time and another had a vicious dog permanently leashed to a tree that barked ferociously at the mower and me.

In the end, dragging the old equipment from one place to the other, plus the cost of gas and the futility of keeping a prehistoric machine running, I didn't have to be an accountant to figure out that I'd be better off doing something else.

Luck had it that a business around the corner needed a part-timer to help load and unload refrigerators in and out of apartment buildings, the majority of which were over ten stories high with no elevators. Some of these old fridges still had compressors on top and weighed as much as a piano, and most were brought into the shop from either junk yards or foreclosures. All, without exception, came with rotten food and maggots that had to be removed prior to sanitizing and reconditioning.

Formed by two blacks and a Cuban, our crew never got tips over fifty cents, and the job required so much heavy lifting that in a matter of days I began to look like Charles Atlas, the physical fitness icon of the nineteen-fifties.

"Many don't like Jevish peeple because ve start with our ass against the vall and end up owning the chop," Sy, the store owner, often said to me. "It's all hard verk and komon sense, Andy. Don't let anyvan mislead *you*. Just remember I vas dare vonce."

Taking upon himself the task of saving my tips, Good Ol' Sy refused to give them back to me until the day I quit for a better job. At that time he handed me a box with five jars full of change: "Don't let yur vife spend it. Remember, dis is only fer yur future bisness."

I have no idea where Good Ol' Sy may be to-day, but his concern and devotion will always be remembered.

Competition in Miami was cut-throat. The un-employment rate in the Cuban community was over fifty percent, and I imagine the blacks were not that far behind, so the thought of leaving Miami began to creep into our minds. In this light we decided to search for better employment all the way from Ev-erglades City north to West Palm Beach and give southern Florida a last chance. I also registered for a course in American taxation at Dade County Jr. College, but realistically, how could anyone accom-plish all this without a car?

As if in the midst of our struggles we needed more excitement, one day Margarita casually told my mother that her nausea had worsened and that she had missed two monthly cycles in a row, some-thing I wasn't even aware of.

Pregnancy rumors reached the ears of our next-door neighbor, and as a nurse practitioner Lisa in-sisted Margarita see a doctor immediately. Alarmed, Papa called Dr. Benitez, a childhood friend from Nuevitas and formerly one of Havana's most pres-tigious gynecologists.

"Have her see me tomorrow first thing in the morning," said Dr. Benitez.

Friday was so slow at the refrigerator company that Good Ol' Sy sent everyone home at noon for a long weekend.

■ ■ ■

"Guess what, Andy?" Margarita welcomes me at the door with a smile that reaches both ears. "You're not going to believe this!"

"I'd believe anything. Why don't you try me?"

"Sit down so you don't fall flat on your face!"

Palpitations take me to sit on the couch with Mama and Papa.

"The doctor said there's nothing wrong with me or my vomiting and that the only reason I'm acting this way is because you and I are going to have a baby!"

"A what? Oh, no, you're not!" I say, horrified.

"Oh, yes, yess, yessss, I am! Doctor Benitez thinks I'm irreversibly pregnant."

"What kind of a joke is this? No woman can be that fertile. He's either crazy, or believes in the breeding qualities of the Holy Spirit. Naaa, I think Papa's friend has lost his mind in exile."

"Have you lost yours?" Mama shoots me an angry stare. "How can you be so cold and indifferent? Give your wife a hug and a kiss and stop acting so selfishly!"

Her direct remarks drive me to the edge.

"You know why the doctor's wrong, Mama? I'll tell you why the doctor is wrong: He's wrong because I don't want to see my baby live under these miserable conditions. He's wrong because the child won't be able to have the best pediatrician in town and because instead of giving birth in a nice hospital my wife will end up in a cheap one run by rookies and rejects. He's wrong because rather than wearing nice maternity dresses, Margarita will be sporting used ones from Goodwill. He's wrong because your grandchild will be playing with hand-me-downs instead of brand new toys. He's wrong because my son or daughter won't be proud of a dad who comes home smelling of sweat and rotten food. God hates Cubans, Mama, and he's punishing the innocent child as well. That's why he's keeping Fidel alive...and that's why the doctor is wrong."

There's a moment of silence.

"He also makes sure every child brings a loaf of bread under his arm," Mama says derisively.

Silence again.

By then Margarita's smile is gone; gone because of my outburst. I know Mother is right; most definitely. I acted like a brute. Yet deep inside I know they understand how I feel.

To make certain her cycles aren't delayed for other reasons, Margarita spends all day Saturday pulling weeds from Lisa's yard and ours, digging trenches to plant flowers we can't afford to buy, edging the lawn three and four times, and to top it off she goes to the kitchen and behind my back drinks a half bottle of brandy accidentally left by Mr. Bolton. All in all, Margarita is doing everything possible to set her body back in sync in case she isn't pregnant.

Tired of plowing in vain, by mid-afternoon she drags me under the avocado tree for a little talk.

Crushing me to her, tears flowing freely, Margarita says softly, "I totally agree with what you said yesterday, Andy, but you must also understand that our lives now more than ever are under God's control, not ours. I know that our financial situation is desperate and a coming baby makes it even worse, but let's also be grateful for our many blessings and stop worrying about the way you smell, or the baby's toys, or the hospital I'll be going to. Let's enjoy the coming of our child as loving parents. And for heaven's sake, stop being so conceited when it comes to accepting help. Just pray that someday you may pass along to others what has been given unto us, and forget everything else."

Pausing for a moment she pulls out one of my hairs.

"Oh, look...a gray one already."

Regardless of conditions Margarita has always

looked at life through a rosy lens, and perhaps because of our Saturday talk under the menacing tree, or maybe because God works in mysterious ways, I awoke the following morning to the most beautiful Sunday in memory, for I saw life through the love and compassion of the woman I loved. Absolutely everything I saw, touched, or smelled had the qualities of a flower—the margarita.

It was such an overwhelming experience that I rushed to the savings jar, and in the absence of credit cards, grabbed forty dollars to take my pregnant wife shopping for all kinds of baby stuff.

Burdines may have gotten most of my savings, but our child was coming on a first-class stork, even if I had to lift, move, and clean double the amount of refrigerators day in and day out.

On Monday, Good Ol Sy tells me that their truck driver fell from a leaky roof over the weekend and couldn't return to work for at least a month.

"You're applying for a chauffeur's license right now." The boss pushes me into the front seat of his brand new Cadillac, where I'll be taking and passing the driving test. In less than two hours I am driving the company truck for an extra dollar an hour. Even though his absence helped me financially, I truly feel sorry for Tommy, the driver.

It suddenly seems as if fortune has taken a turn for the better. Next, Cousin Pedrito calls and tells me that one of his refugee neighbors is buying a newer car and that the dealer flatly refused to accept his 1949 DeSoto convertible as a trade-in. By then all we had in the piggy bank were fifty dollars to buy groceries.

Pedrito takes me to see the hand-painted vehicle.

Different coats of yellows are evident in areas badly scorched by the hot Florida sun, and the floor is so corroded and delaminated that we can see the asphalt underneath. I could possibly stop the car with my own two feet if necessary.

"Since it uses a lot of water, you must fill up the radiator every morning, which of course is no big deal," says Roberto, the owner.

"Does it use oil?" I ask.

Pedrito shrugs. "Who cares if it uses oil, Andy, for Christ's sake? It's only a dime for a quart of bulk."

"That's okay, let him ask. Yes, it uses about a quart every five hundred miles, and again that's no big deal," says Roberto.

"How come the front bumper leans so much to the right?"

"That's because the left rear tire is larger than the others; again, no big deal."

"Is it stick or automatic?"

"It's neither. You select the car's three speeds by backing off the accelerator pedal every time you need to shift gears."

"Mmm, and where's the button that moves the roof back and forth?"

"There's no button, *mi hermano*; your wife grabs one side and you the other. It's that simple. No gadgets and no electricity to run down your battery. Also no big deal."

Stroking his whiskers, Roberto cagily looks at the car. *"Mira, chico, si lo que tu quieres es transporte, no pierdas mas tiempo mirando. Aqui esta tu carro!* (Look, buddy, if all you want is reliable transportation, don't waste your time looking around, because this is the car.) Besides, have you ever heard of a convertible selling for a hundred dollars?"

"But I don't have the hundred. All I have is twenty-five bucks...I'm sorry."

"Fifty! I'd let you have it for fifty. How's that for a deal?"

"I'm going to have a baby and need the money to pay doctors and buy stuff, so at this moment that's all I can afford," I say almost apologetically.

"Mmm. How about twenty-five down and twenty-five in two months?"

"Oh, no, it's not only the money. It's that a car without a floor is too dangerous to drive with a child inside. Can you imagine an innocent little baby falling through that huge crack out there?"

207

Like in Havana, when a couple of men argue in public, ten others join in and take sides, so before long, eight of Roberto's neighbors are witnessing the ludicrous bargaining match.

"The car is just a piece of crap, Roberto," says the loudest of the bunch. "It's a running miracle. For goodness sake, let him have it, or you'll end up paying someone to take it off your hands."

A hairy guy in shorts and *chancletas* winks mischievously. *"Oye, Viejo, por Dios; ten compasion,* the man's pregnant! Didn't he say he was going to have a baby?"

Hugging his beer-belly to keep the laughter from hurting, Roberto eyes me with tears of joy. *"Mire, compadre,* I'll do anything for a pregnant man, even if he's Pedrito's friend."

Handing me the key with one hand, Roberto grabs the money with the other—twenty-five bucks.

"Olvidate del papeleo, y no me vengas arriba si te vas por el agujero pa bajo. Forget the paperwork and don't come after me if you fall down the hole."

I yell at the audience from the rolled-down window of my yellow submarine. "Hey, *mi gente.* Pregnant or not, I look great inside this thing, don't I?"

It was short of miraculous to see fate intervene on behalf of the grateful poor: Twice the salary for an entire month, a free driver's license, and a twenty-five-dollar convertible, all in less than a week.

Piled up outside the hardware store, various pieces of plywood await the trash man; grabbing a few on my way home, I manage to install a wooden floor in the car, thanks to Mr. Bolton's antiquated tools. Furthermore, a remnant outlet one block away has thrown pieces of carpet on the sidewalk, so I pick out some fancy ones from the pile and cover the entire floor with a flowery design that eventually my wife comes to hate with a passion. Repainting the body in a more subdued yolky yellow becomes my next project. After all, why not add the art of brush-painting a car to the many self-taught skills learned to survive poverty in exile?

The miraculous DeSoto stayed with us a little over a year. It took us everywhere we wanted, and the only cost besides gas was a rebuilt battery. Luckily the hundreds of gallons of tap water were absolutely free. Since we couldn't afford to replace the tires, the large one on the rear kept our De Soto, as Lisa's boyfriend would put it: "Listing on the starboard side as if it wanted to roll into the ocean."

CHAPTER 24

The Search Begins

Our phone rings in the middle of night.

"Oye, Andy, es Eladio. Te acuerdas de mi?"

The law professor from the sausage company is calling me during his midnight coffee break.

"Luis quit his job this morning and the boss asked him to recommend another Cuban to replace him. Do you want to hear about it?"

"Of course I do."

"They pay $60.00 a week plus hospital insurance after ninety days and a week's vacation every year. But I'm not too sure you'd be interested in this kind of work."

"Heck, it can't be worse than what I'm doing now. The pay is much better and the health insurance is definitely a plus; so tell me about it."

"It's at the McGowen Mortuary on S.W. Eighth Street. You still want me to continue?"

"Yes," I say, dropping my voice.

"All I can tell you is that it's basically janitorial."

"Janitorial, eh?"

There's a long pause:

"Dime la verdad, te interesa, o no?"

"Yes, of course, I'm definitely interested. Tell me who I'm supposed to see and when."

"The funeral director's name is George Raft— like the movie star. He's there every morning at eight-thirty including Sundays, so I'd suggest you show up around eight and introduce yourself as a good friend of Luis Lopez's family. Don't dress too casually, and remember to act piously. Honestly, Andy, I think you'd make a hell of a good impression."

I'm up to shower at seven and dress in black and gray for the gloomy interview.

"You can't go to work like that!" says Margarita. Those are your best pants, are you crazy? Take them off!"

I hadn't planned to tell her about Eladio's offer

until I got back from the mortuary, but she insists. When I explain, she laughs.

"*Tu, trabajando para una funeraria?* (You, working for a mortuary?) I'll bet Eladio was pulling your leg. Why don't you call him right now and make sure he wasn't joking?"

Agreeing that the worst effort is the one that's never made, Margarita concedes that in all fairness to Eladio I should talk to Mr. Raft; so at eight-thirty I'm knocking at the door of the McGowen Mortuary in Little Havana.

Wearing a nurse's uniform, an albino lady in her mid-fifties opens the door and tells me that guest visitation won't start until ten. After I explain the reason for my call, she asks me to wait in the lobby for Mr. Raft. I'm stunned by the woman's Martian appearance.

The leather couch is stiff and cold as a corpse. Atop a glass table a huge flower arrangement adds a scent of lilacs to the opulent surroundings. On the wall behind it hangs a heavily carved Belgian frame with the oil painting of a man in black whose face flawlessly resembles the husband in Grant Wood's famous "American Gothic."

I'm sure that socio is—or was—one of the founders, I think.

Complementing the sanctimonious mood, astutely concealed speakers disperse the organ music of J.S. Bach. The sound is projected so transparently throughout the entire area that only an audiophile could deny its heavenly origins.

"Señor Rodriguez, Mr. Raft would like to see you now," the woman in white says solemnly.

I'll bet she came to Miami on a flying saucer, I think.

Walking to the funeral director's office, I notice small booths on both sides of the hall. Each cubicle has three chairs, a podium with a guest book, and an open coffin awaiting its refrigerated guest to arrive shortly before ten.

I'm beginning to feel the portentous surroundings weighing on me and the breakfast of *gofio con café con leche (*toasted wheat with caffe-latte) churning inside my tummy like cement in a concrete mixer.

Finally I meet Mr. Raft, a tall man who must weigh at least three hundred pounds. A black suit, black tie, and a starchy white shirt, the cuffs of which have links the size of Krugerrands, give the man an affluent and solemn look, and his hair—too black and bushy to be his— reminds me of the day I accidentally spilled an entire bottle of India ink across my sixth grade teacher's desk.

Curiously enough and perhaps due to the preserving qualities of formaldehyde, the mortician's seventy-two- year-old-face shows no signs of wear and tear; yet the mere effort of standing up and shaking hands leaves the man huffing and puffing like a derby horse.

"Please sit down, Mr. Rodriguez," says the wheezing executive.

I cheerfully invent the answer to his first question—how long have I known the Lopez family. Then, with downcast eyes he poses others irrelevant to the job.

His questions are so meticulously crafted that I wonder why a janitorial position in a mortuary would require so much scrutiny. Then I realize that since most applicants have never been around the dead and a long and costly training is essential, Mr. Raft wants to ensure that I have the right gut to fit the mold.

Annoyed by the fact that Mr. Raft is constantly trying to avoid eye contact, I begin to take things with a grain of salt, a tad of fear, and a carload of suspicion.

"If you agree with the conditions I'm going to set forth, Mr. Rodriguez, you can consider yourself hired."

If my stomach churned before, now it is on fire. The Cuban breakfast Margarita has been serving of late isn't exactly mortuary friendly.

"You will work eight-hour days, six days a week except during flu season, when overtime becomes the rule. In that case we pay time and a half.

"Even though you'll be hired as a janitor, Mr. Rodriguez, the word is a bit misleading. I want you to know that there are other duties besides keeping the place clean."

"C-can you give me an example?" I stammer.

"I certainly will. For instance, while our guests remain refrigerated, body fluids may drip into the receptacles overnight, so your first assignment every morning will be to clean and sterilize these basins. You'll also be maintaining the embalming equipment and making sure there are enough chemicals in stock to cover an overload. I would also require you to assist our artists, embalmers, and craftsmen in their individual duties as necessary and to perform as told, and without hesitation

"You will also help Miss Dart, the lady in white, to make sure that every guest is placed in the right room and in the right coffin before ten A.M., and you shall also help her dress and undress the bodies--"

Mr. Raft suddenly comes to complete stop. "Well, we don't call them bodies anymore. We call them guests. So please remember: guests—not corpses, not stiffs, not bodies; just guests."

I nod dutifully.

"And very important, Mr Rodriguez: Courtesy, silence, and above all an air of solemnity are mandatory throughout our premises at all times. Joking is not allowed. If you want to laugh, go to the toilet, and if someone asks you any kind of question other than where the restrooms are, you will direct them to Miss Dart.

"We'll pay you sixty dollars a week during the first three months, increasing to sixty-five thereafter. At that time you'll become eligible to join our health insurance and prepaid funeral expense plans. We'll also provide with you a suit like mine, which the mortuary will dry clean weekly at its own expense. But you'll be responsible for the white shirts and black shoes. Oh, and you'll be entitled to a week's paid vacation every twelve months.

"If in ninety days you're as lovesick as I am with this business, I'd strongly recommend you join our seminars and make a career of our unassuming profession.

"Please read this contract, Mr. Rodriguez, and sign it at the bottom so you can start on Monday." Mr. Raft presses on decisively.

"Er, Mr. Raft, I would like to share this proposal with my wife before making a commitment," I say. Would it be all right if I take the papers home and call you tomorrow morning with an answer?"

"Most definitely." Gasping for air, the funeral director leads me to the front door.

Driving home from the creepy premises I realize that perhaps for an ambitious person with a stainless steel stomach, the opportunity to grow at McGowen would be irresistible. I'm convinced that Mr. Raft is pretty darn close to joining the guest list himself.

"I'd rather starve to death before I see you working for *a funeraria*!" With asteroidal force Margarita stamps her elegant foot on our twenty-year-old carpet.

"I don't want to hear about it! I don't care what they have offered you, and I also don't care if I have to become a maid to help out with expenses, but you will not, and I repeat will *not* work as a mortician."

"Hey, calm down. I'm only telling the story to see what you think."

Hands on her hips, Margarita softens her tone:

"Can you imagine our after-dinner conversations? 'Oh, honey, it was virtually impossible to make the boy look real. She lost control when his coffin was closed. Oh, my God, you should've seen the hole in his head.' And every night, Andy, every single night, you'll be dwelling on the macabre until sooner or later a dark cloud sets permanently over your head...and mine, of course. Life's colors will darken, and if you're worried sick about our baby's response to the smell of sweat and rotten food, imagine his reaction to human flesh and formaldehyde. That's a job for the depressed, Andy, not for you. Definitely not for you."

"'Assistant zoo-keeper needed at the Primate Jungle Park. Good pay, fringe benefits, $1.50 hr.' Why not give the apes a shot?" Margarita says, clipping the ad. "It's better to work with monkeys than with corpses, don't you agree?"

Offering benefits similar to McGowen's, the job consists of brushing and feeding the apes, cleaning their cells, and keeping the landscape green and luscious; but there is also a catch, or it wouldn't have made it to the classifieds.

As I am told in the interview, infatuated with his own feces, a two-hundred-pound gorilla likes to pitch his poop at the spectators and rub his hands on himself afterwards. Therefore the candidate chosen for the job has to clean the cell bars, the floors, the walls, the ceilings, and bathe and brush the ape every single morning before nine.

Needless to say, there are no arguments here.

Soon thereafter I am waiting in the lobby of the Americana Hotel to interview for a bookkeeping position. Three hours later someone tells the fifty applicants that the position has been filled. The lucky fellow has a business degree from a correspondence school, speaks perfect English, and was recommended by one of the Americana's oldest employees. So much for a coat and tie job; so much for my college degree.

During this time I also manage to land another

part-time job, from four in the afternoon to eight at night. It is the cleanest so far, but it only pays a dollar an hour. All I have to do is copy from the county clerk's office the names and addresses of new home buyers—lists that my boss will sell in sticker-format to furniture stores, insurance companies, and so on, as prospective customers.

In spite of living in poverty and at the mercy of a labor market that may never turn around, we are also blessed in many ways. According to Dr.Benitez, Margarita is having a perfect pregnancy. We already have four hundred dollars in the kitty, an honest reason to consider giving up our financial help. And our legal status is changed from "free on parole" to "immigrant residents." I never thought it possible until then that a person could love and pledge allegiance to one country and have his heart set in another at the same time.

"Mr. and Mrs. Rodriguez, I wouldn't recommend you stop the economic aid at this point," says our courteous social worker. "With a baby on the way I'm sure you'll be needing the extra money, and if we cut it off it'll be almost impossible to reinstate it in case of need. I urge you sit tight and wait for relocation, because even though the number of applications is huge, there are also hundreds of religious organizations all over the U.S. willing to sponsor Cuban families—so I'm pretty sure your chances of going places before the end of the year are pretty darn good. Just be patient."

"What about health care for my wife and baby?"

"Don't worry, Mr. Rodriguez, we've got you covered."

And boy, was the lady right! Within a week Margarita's boss at Jackson Byron's lays her off because their liability insurance won't cover pregnant employees.

At the time, Pipo was also in Miami. Mima and Grandpa had decided to stay behind and wait for Castro to be deposed or assassinated; but as it always happens, the more one wishes a tormenter's extermination, the longer the person seems to live. I wondered why, with so many Castro-like gems cluttering human history, one of them hadn't already achieved eternal life.

Business executives and many professionals had managed to transfer their degrees and skills to the United States. Lawyers like Pipo, however, had nothing to offer except their own stories, so they either got jobs like Eladio's or ended up catering meals home to home like Margarita's father—a far cry from being Havana's most reputable labor attorney.

Early one morning our phone rang:

"I'm in a pickle, Andy," the sticker boss cried desperately. "I need you to work at least ten hours straight to help me out of this mess."

The snag: it was Friday the thirteenth, the wickedest of days to break routines, drive fast, get married, or leave home. It was also Margarita's father day off—and auspiciously the one chosen by his daughter to go into labor.

Shortly after I left for work, she began to sense that something inside her wasn't right. Alone in the house she called Pipo for help, and in minutes they were on their way to Mercy Hospital.

Meanwhile, working inside the Dade County vault, I had no idea of what was happening in the outside world. So much for being by my wife's side at one of life's greatest moments.

According to Margarita, the emergency room was a crowded loony bin, and they didn't even allow her father to be by her side, only husbands; so poor Pipo had to stay behind feeling like a nervous wreck...waiting.

Her labor pains increased and the only intern who wasn't attending a life-threatening situation at the moment was a rookie who looked like a teenager and did not speak Spanish.

"Can you wait until I find a real obstetrician?" he asked.

In the intense pain only mothers can appreciate, scared, alone, and at the mercy of whatever came her way, Margarita delivered our first baby assisted by the novice, who according to Dr. Benitez—out-of-town that Friday the thirteenth—did worse than anyone standing on the sidewalk.

Other than my poor wife feeling like the pennies on the Nuevitas railroad track, our 9 ½ lb. baby boy was born with a dimple in his chin—my family's trademark—and as healthy as we had prayed for.

Four days later the two were on their way home, where Lisa waited to teach Margarita everything about nursing and caring for a newborn. Luck also had it that the pediatrician who had taken care of me as a kid was now in Miami; thus he became little Andy's doctor. Like Dr.Benitez, Dr. Silva adamantly refused to charge for his services. Thanks to better values in those days, tort law didn't interfere with a physician's oath to serve his patients regardless of health insurance and pocket depth.

In early October the nearly forgotten social worker from the refugee center called again:

"Mrs. Rodriguez, there's an opportunity for relocation in Las Vegas, and I wonder if you'd be interested? Otherwise there are hundreds waiting to settle in that city. I honestly think it's a horrible place to raise a family, but I'm supposed to tell you anyway. What would you like me to do?"

Her honesty, and the fact she was absolutely right, made us decline the offer. By then, my wife had already gone back to her original size and we were one poor, but very happy family.

Shortly thereafter, Dolores's daughter Nancy and her husband Mario paid us a visit. He had been hired to a much better position in Puerto Rico and came to offer me his old job as a provisions deliveryman in the Florida Keys, with Key West as a home base.

Considering it was a dead-end job in a town then as bad as Las Vegas in which to raise a family, I wasn't eager to take the bait.

"Even if the job pays well, I don't particularly care to live so close to Cuba," I complained to Margarita. "It's just a gut feeling and I don't like it."

"If they've been kind enough to offer you the job, the least we can do is spend a day or two with them in the keys. Otherwise it'll be very impolite," Margarita replies, in her infinite wisdom, telling me off.

At their insistence, and to learn first-hand what the job entailed, and to avoid being rude, we agreed to spend a couple of days at their Key West apartment along with the baby.

The morning following our arrival, October 12, 1962, the Cuban Missile Crisis exploded in all its dramatic intensity, catching us within shooting range of Castro's missiles. It felt as though I had successfully escaped bondage to plummet into my own trap.

Running away from Cuba's terror and encountering it again in the US was too much for me to bear. *Maldito sea!! *-!#*! Damn, damn, damn!*

By noon, stores were out of bottled water, flashlights, canned foods, candles, and everything a prudent person would hoard under a hurricane warning.

The in-bound lane of the only road connecting the keys to the mainland was closed to allow hundreds of missile launchers to arrive from the base in Homestead. The next day the entire coastline was dotted with them.

Open trucks crammed with soldiers came and went as people in the streets watched in disbelief. The relentless noise of jet planes flying overhead was the only sound that made us feel protected. "There goes John Wayne in his jet fighter," I say to Mario.

Inconceivable as it may sound, the small town of Key West was preparing for a preemptive missile attack from Cuba. Hard to believe? Not in those days.

After delivering groceries for an entire day to stores that had run out of everything, I ruefully told Mario that I wasn't going to settle within that lunatic's shooting distance. "If need be, I'd rather live on the moon."

"But how could you let an opportunity like this go down the toilet?" Mario shrugged, opening his palms. "Can't you see this is the end of Fidel Castro? Come on, Andy, open your eyes, man, *El loco ese* is challenging the most powerful country on earth! His hours are numbered."

"For Christ's sake, Mario, if Kennedy didn't have the guts to come forward during the Bay of Pigs, do you really believe he's going to start a nuclear war on account of Fidel Castro? Come on, *mi socio*, wake up!"

To coerce the Russians to pull out their long-range missiles from the Alligator Island, President Kennedy launched a naval blockade to prevent ships from reaching Cuban ports. But the siege didn't last long. In the end, the Soviet Union agreed to withdraw their missiles on condition that the US would never invade the island or assist in subversive activities against it. In short, the gamble worked, and the Soviets got what they wanted without firing a shot: the establishment of a communist puppet regime ninety miles away from the United States.

As far as freedom-loving Cubanos were concerned, however, the October Missile Crisis drove the last nail into the Alligator Island's coffin. May it rest in peace.

Guilt-ridden for wasting Mario's and Nancy's valuable time, and upset for putting our safety in jeopardy, we drove home the following day.

What a fiasco, the entire episode. On our way back, in an intuitive attempt to protect Andy from an "inevitable" missile attack, Margarita couldn't cover him with enough blankets and stuff. She was panic-stricken and the boy was suffocating.

"This is the last time you ask me to do something against my instincts." Mad as hell, I shifted the DeSoto into third gear.

"You shouldn't feel angry," Margarita replied. "They did it with their best intentions. Besides, who would have known?"

In three hours we reached Miami through S.W.8th Street. Little Havana was on fire; not exactly in flames, but in a sizzling frenzy. From Le Jeune Road east to 12th Avenue, the well-known street had more Cubanos arguing and screaming in the middle of the road than in Havana during baseball playoffs.

Cuban and American flags fluttered in the wind of Miami's first cold front. Chilly as it was, a produce market offered free coconut water and frosty *guarapo* (freshly-squeezed cane juice) to pedestrians in anticipation of a free Cuba. Cars honked their horns, and in a corner lot known as the "domino capital of the world" the old and the unemployed argued, wigwagged, and played. Farther down the street, suitably located loudspeakers relayed the latest news according to *Radio Bemba, or* Radio

Lips—the funny name given to a Spanish station that kept many Cubanos on edge thinking they would be returning to Cuba the following day.

"What if the Marines are already in Havana and we don't know it?" Said Margarita. "This car definitely needs a radio."

"Perhaps we're driving through another insane asylum and they know something we don't."

The phone rang as we opened the door:

"Mrs. Rodriguez, I have just received a request from a Lutheran church in Denver to sponsor a couple and a child. I have talked to the pastor, and to tell you the truth, Mrs. Rodriguez, this one is going to be hard to beat. Would you like me to investigate more?"

CHAPTER 25
The Promised Land

Carrying a huge diaper bag and a box full of baby outfits embroidered by Mima and smuggled through the mail, we landed in Denver on November 3, 1962. Our other assets-the car, the crib, and a window fan—stayed in Miami in case we had to return with our tails between our legs.

Simple and unpretentious, the airport suggested a small western town—stagecoach, saloon, and the whole bit—instead of a city as beautiful as Colorado's capital. Those were the days when the stockyards east of the airfield told stories of cattle trains,

Buffalo Bill, and Molly Brown, and of westerns in which good guys never lost.

"The skies are the bluest I've ever seen and at night they're so translucent that stars seem to shine at arm's length," I wrote my father. "And the mountains, Dad, you should see those gorgeous Rockies, studded with Christmas trees year round; aspens, Douglas firs, and blue spruces growing in air so thin locals say it comes in short pants. Can you imagine Christmas ad infinitum? What a nightmare!"

"You're drinking the freshest water and breathing the purest air in America, Andy," Ed, one of my future co-workers, would say to me once. "Don't forget this is God's country."

Since God had already determined that we should enjoy two of his greatest masterpieces, the ocean blue and the Rocky Mountains, our new home in Colorado tied with Gulf and Atlantic beaches in our perception of the Promised Land.

As members of the St. Mark Lutheran Church in Applewood, a small Community west of Denver, Carl Smith, his wife Sonya, and son Charlie, awaited our arrival.

All I remember from that landing are the airport, the stockyards, the skies, and the love and warmth shown three strangers by a generous family and their church; selfless people with no ulterior motive but sharing their humanity with us. These Americans with hearts of gold assumed responsibility for a family of three as if we were their own. *Ay, la buena suerte, tan lejos y a la vez tan cerca.* Oh, Fortuna! Seemingly so remote...yet, at hand.

The car passes by the Purina Dog Chow silo en route to North Denver, and in exactly fifteen minutes it turns south onto Sheridan Blvd. across from the Lakeside Amusement Park, the second-most exciting place of entertainment in those days after Elitch Gardens.

Are they taking us to their home, an apartment, a hotel...a hole on the ground? I wonder. Four more turns and Carl parks in front of a small house surrounded by so many ash and maple trees that their fallen leaves could easily fill up the entire dwelling.

Carl opens the door. The modest living room appears to have been decorated by Mother Goose and furnished by Baby Bear. Ahead of the small kitchen a dinette table stands, with a vase full of fresh zinnias and two place settings on top. On my left there's a closet stocked with brooms, a vacuum cleaner, detergents, dusters, and lots of rags, and on my right another one full of linens, towels, tablecloths, napkins, aprons, blankets, and so on. And as a nostalgic reminder of my childhood years, in front of me stands the same kind of G.E. refrigerator my family had when I was a kid.

Atop the kitchen counter, a topless breadbox is

packed with Gerber jars, and underneath, cabinet drawers are crammed with enough gadgets to fit every culinary fancy. The only thing missing in the entire house is a flickering neon sign saying: Welcome home!

In the bedroom a crib and a bed are already made. The crib has rattles dangling from the rail, and down on the floor, an open chest full of brand new toys precariously awaits Andy's discovery.

We're dumfounded. Even our child is still. *How could these people love strangers this much? That's impossible!* I think. *How could anyone share so much with creatures from an alien world? Is it possible that after so many nightmares I am beginning to dream?*

"Andy, do you have any money?" Carl cuts into my thoughts.

"Yes sir, I have four hundred dollars."

"Please don't spend it. Our church will take care of your financial needs until you get settled."

"Can we stay in this house? How much is the rent?" I ask timidly.

"You certainly can. I just bought it to make sure your family had a secure and decent place to live. As far as rent is concerned, wait until you can afford to pay me fifty dollars a month; meanwhile, don't worry about it, for we don't need the money."

"You mean you and your wife bought this house

to rent it to us for fifty dollars a month?"

"That's exactly right. I'm sure someday it'll pay off."

"But sir...I mean, Carl; how could it be a good investment with a rent like that?

"Just because the rent is low doesn't mean it's a poor investment. Besides, this one is special."

"But Carl--"

"No more ifs and buts, Andy. Come and let me show you how to operate the furnace, the humidifier, and the washing machine."

"Why do we need a humidifier?"

"Because there's little moisture in the air at this altitude. You come from a very humid environment, and we wanted to make sure no one would suffer nosebleeds. Besides, you'll be much more comfortable this way."

Following Carl to the back porch, I marvel at a tiny garage behind the house. What a neat place to hide and build stuff.

"When the load is finished," he points at a spigot under the tub, "open this valve, drain it, and pass each garment through the wringer on top at least twice. I'm sorry we couldn't find you a better washer and a dryer, so until then use the clothesline. And remember—always bring the diapers inside before they freeze."

With so many topics to talk about we sit in the

tiny living room and chat almost till midnight.

They ask us about life under communism, our ordeal leaving the country, relatives left behind, our feelings about America, the Cuban Missile Crisis, and the Bay of Pigs fiasco. To my surprise, in spite of living in the center of the country, Carl and Sonya understand very clearly the dilemmas created in Latin America by US foreign policy.

"If Castro's regime collapses tomorrow, would you go back to Cuba?" Sonya asks.

"To escape was very difficult." I reply. "To risk doing it again would be sheer insanity on our part, and I for one don't want my children ever to experience the same horrendous nightmare. We're grateful to America for their welcome. Our firstborn is a US citizen and so will be the rest of our family. Here they'll have a fair chance at a stable life and a decent future. No, madam, I will not return."

"But we would definitely go visit," Margarita eagerly chimes in.

So absorbed were Sonya and Carl in our issues that we decided to postpone our hundred questions for a more suitable time.

"Can we pick you up tomorrow around nine-thirty?" Carl stands up to leave. "Our service starts at ten, and everyone's dying to meet you."

"We'd love to meet them too," says Margarita, a wide grin lighting her features.

CHAPTER 26

The Grange Hall

"Have you two had breakfast?" asks Sonya.

"We overslept, so we only had juice."

"Then why don't you join us for lunch and a short ride to the mountains after the service?"

"Oh, we'd love to," Margarita says joyfully.

On our way to the Applewood church we pass by small farms selling fresh milk, eggs, honey, and the yummiest corn in the world. There are still pumpkin patches here and there, and orchards with luscious red apples all along the small farming community road. The air is crisp and the colors of late fall sharper under the early morning sun.

"You won't miss the Florida sun, Andy. I promise. Denver has more sunny days than any southern city, including Miami." Sonya tries to make us to feel at home in colorful Colorado.

"How cold does it get here?" I ask the good lady.

"It may go down to thirty below zero, but always under a shining sun."

"Did you know that the coldest city in the US is in Colorado?" Carl interjects.

"And wh-where is this place?"

"The town's name is Fraser and it is in the mountains ten miles west of Winter Park."

Margarita and I look at each other in wonder. No more questions about climate.

"Welcome to our church!" says Carl, stopping in front of a barnlike building with the sign "Applewood Grange Hall" on top.

Leased from the local farmers by Pastor Bob and his Lutheran congregation, the building is large enough to accommodate the regional growers' association, but not St. Mark's entire congregation of about sixty families. Pastor Bob's dream is to build a new church in the Applewood community some day, and even though plans are already underway, the limited number of members makes the financial restrictions cumbersome. The mere thought of the congregation putting their commitment aside to care for us makes me feel as puny as my baby's thumb.

Pastor Bob and his wife Shirley welcome us at the entrance; by then the hall is filled to capacity, and as we walk to our reserved seats in the front row, I get the impression that everyone is shocked at how young we are to be in such a mess. I'm twenty-three, Margarita twenty, and the baby four months old. All together we don't add to forty-four.

In his opening remarks the pastor welcomes us as St. Mark's very special guests, and he asks us to stand up for a round of applause—something unheard of in Cuban churches in those days. The good folks scrutinize us from head to toe. I've never felt so out of place in my entire life.

The piano player concludes Bach's "Jesu, Joy of Man's Desiring," and the service begins.

Suddenly, either scared by the pastor's voice or bothered by gas, Little Andy decides to throw a fit.

"It's gas, my dear, it's only gas. Oh, poor thing." The lady behind us pats Margarita's shoulder.

"Tap him, tap him on the back," says the one next to her.

Fresh as the morning frost, young Mama listens to everyone's advice on how to bring the baby under control.

"Do you mind if I hold him for a second? I have ten grandchildren, you know," says a woman sitting by Carl and Sonya.

"You two may have another Mario Lanza in the family," says the husband of the lady who offered the gas diagnosis.

Andy's temper continues to heat up until the liturgy is about to collapse. Then, for reasons short of miraculous, the child finally shuts up. The religious mood returns to normal, and I wish I were an ostrich with a pile of sand under my chair.

The pastor speaks of tyranny and oppression in other countries, the threat of radicalism to Christianity and to the Free World, and America's responsibility to come forward before it is too late. By mid-sermon he addresses us directly:

"Mr. and Mrs. Rodriguez, no matter how much you think you're receiving, please bear in mind that you're giving us much, much more, for you have brought into our midst a sense of dignity and courage...and a sacred reminder that if America is to survive, the religious and moral duty of all Christians is to join and assist those who, like you, refuse to accept evil as a way of life."

Margarita is in tears. Her English is rough, but she understands what Pastor Bob is saying.

Never praised in front of an audience, I choose to become self-conscious instead.

The sermon over, everyone stands up for communion.

"Shouldn't we follow?" I whisper.

"We're Catholics, don't you remember?" replies Margarita.

"So? What difference does it make? Come on, let's go up front. That's the least we can do."

As we move forward I wonder how my old catechism teacher, Ms. Suarez, would have evaluated the situation. "No more tickets for the Auditorium, Andy. No more tickets!" Or more likely: "Well done, Andy, well done. I'm glad you've learned that God is everywhere."

Afterwards Pastor Bob invites the entire congregation to "join together and welcome this courageous couple after the service, for their ordeal is indeed worthy of commendation."

He spreads his arms open wide. "May the Lord bless thee and keep thee; may the Lord shine his light upon thee and bring you peace. May He also bless the Rodriguezes as they begin a new life in America, and may He always keep our country in the palm of His hand, in the name of Jesus Christ, our Lord, Amen. The service has ended. Go in peace."

In the basement, everyone's lining up to meet the "daring refugees". There are cookies and refreshments, and even though Margarita doesn't understand much of what's being said, she manages to carry on and even start some new friendships. For the first time in years my self-esteem gets a boost as I begin to feel like a hero instead of a hobo, and as more invitations to dinners and gatherings crowd our schedule.

Compliments to the "handsome baby and his gorgeous outfit" come from every woman in the congregation, and although his mama doesn't understand everything they say, she knows darn well they're admiring the child and Mima's masterpieces.

Meanwhile, I'm also amazed at the gift of Cuban women to express themselves without words. Contrary to *los machos Cubanos,* who wouldn't gesture in front of others for fear of being called *afeminados*, Cuban women don't mind talking and arguing with their hands, as well as every movable part of their body, in order to communicate.

In his late sixties, tall, broad-shouldered, and walking with a cane, Mr. Thompson, an injured WWII veteran, hands me an envelope with a fifty-dollar bill inside.

"Oh, no please...I can't."

"*Si, señor, por favor;* take *it,*" he expresses in heavily accented Spanish. "It's been a family tradition for generations, and all I ask is that you pass it down someday to someone like you, for that's what makes our country great."

The pastor and his wife, Shirley, take a back

seat during the gathering, and as the crowd dwindles, Shirley invites us to dinner at their home the following day so we can meet their daughters, Laurie and Carol, and learn more of each other.

Following the lively reception we join Carl, Sonya, and their young son Charlie for lunch at the Village Inn, where I treat my neglected stomach to quality pancakes it hasn't had in ages. Carl takes us for a mountain ride all the way to North-Pole-Fraser, where temperatures are a warm thirty degrees and the sun is shining. Colorado is beautiful, no doubt about it.

We get of the car for a cup of coffee, and I can't stop staring at the gutsy townspeople, their homes and their cars. *Are these folks normal? How can they survive this place?* I wonder.

To watch skiing for the first time, we visit the small town of Winter Park on our way home, stop at the small train station to show Andy a locomotive, and cross the continental divide through Berthoud Pass—twelve thousand feet above Castroland.

Thank God, he's way below and his missiles far behind. I sigh with relief.

Carl looks tired. He has been mountain-driving for over four hours.

"What else can we show them on the way back?" he asks his wife.

"Let's drive through Lookout Mountain so they

can see the city lights and visit Buffalo Bill's grave," Sonya suggests.

"The next time we should drive them to Central City and Black Hawk. Both are cowboy towns with saloons, stables, a gold mine, and the whole bit," adds their son Charlie, who has been very quiet during the entire trip.

We arrive home around eight. Our rapport is great and the journey to the mountains absolutely delightful, notwithstanding the "air that comes in short pants."

Tuesday morning Carl phones me on his way to work.

"Whenever you're ready, Andy, I'd like you to meet a couple of friends. One's an accountant for Mile High Truck and Equipment, and the other one a manager for a credit union."

"What about tomorrow morning?"

"Tomorrow morning is fine. I'll pick you up at eight."

Shirley arrives with her daughters, Laurie and Carol.

"I have errands to run and I'm also taking Laurie to the pediatrician. Would you like to come and meet him?"

She takes us to the Lakewood Medical Center, the lobby of which is packed with sick kids, some with diarrhea, others with green boogers running down their noses, all crying.

Suffering an ear infection, Laurie is the quietest of all and the last one to be called. Margarita and I wait outside with little Carol.

"The Rodriguez family; please follow me, " one of the nurses finally announces.

We pass by a dozen cubicles, all with terrified children crying their hearts out.

"That's why I wanted to be a surgeon, see? All of them would be anesthetized by now," I whisper to Margarita.

Inside the crowded little office we sit two to a chair, next to Shirley and Laurie, waiting.

Followed by a nurse, a young, pleasant-looking man in a white coat enters. The nurse hands him a notepad and a stethoscope. "Mr. and Mrs. Rodriguez, sorry I couldn't meet you last Sunday, but I was on call. I'm Dr. Miller, another member of St. Marks."

Taking time from his hectic schedule, the busy Dr. Miller sits on a stool and chats about everything except children and disease. Bob, Shirley, and he are good friends and he obviously needs a break. Dr. Miller looks drained, and his day has just begun.

"Please let me take care of the little boy. It'll be a privilege to be a part of this wonderful effort." Stroking Andy's hair he gazes at us over his sagging eyeglasses.

We nod our assent, and the good doctor lays the baby on a table, examines him, orders a couple of vaccines, and hands Margarita a bagful of free samples and a feeding plan.

On the threshold, Dr. Miller whispers, his arm around my shoulder, "Please don't worry about fees or prescriptions, okay? We'll talk about all that some other time."

As agreed, at eight the next morning Carl is knocking on our door.

"Our first call will be Mile High Truck, Andy, the place where the comptroller is a friend of mine."

Showing us their massive retrofitting facilities and talking about everything but a job opening, Carl's friend promises to keep me posted of any future changes. Meanwhile, looking out the window, I'm mesmerized by the first snowstorm of the season. What a sight...snow! And what a disappointment...no job.

At the credit union, Carl's friend is out to lunch and someone else has already been hired for the bookkeeping position. Here, we don't even pass beyond the receptionist. All in all the entire morning is a waste of time and a letdown to both of us.

At home, Margarita is getting ready to go shopping for an alarm clock and a copy of the *Denver Post.*

"Let's go try our first snowstorm together," she

says, all excited. "You'll feel much better by the time we come back. Oh, how I wish we had a camera."

"How can we spend money on a camera when our only coats are the ones bought at Goodwill in Miami? We'll buy one soon, I promise."

Wet and heavy, the snow looks like goose down. We stretch our arms to see it melt on our jackets, and Margarita opens her mouth to catch a flake here and there. Little Andy is deeply serious, because after all, he'd rather be in the tropics.

Next morning at eight I begin calling and making appointments from the classifieds, and since I don't want to bother Shirley or Carl, I always take the bus and walk. The routine goes on for about a month; applications, interviews, phone calls, and rejections...many, many rejections.

And every day without fail, Shirley and Margarita run errands together. Shirley picks up Margarita in the morning and brings her back around three, after an entire day of exposure to our newly adopted culture. This occurs all in English, because Shirley doesn't know Spanish, so in less than three grueling months my wife is speaking the language almost fluently and they have become very good friends.

On December second I call the Board of Water Commissioners for an interview regarding a newspaper ad for a junior accountant.

On December fourth I meet with the comptroller

and the Chief Accountant at their downtown offices. The meeting is pleasant, and I feel at ease, because the topics are primarily focused on my life as an individual rather than as a professional. In fact, I present them with a microfilm of my accounting degree they don't even look at. The interview lasts a little over an hour and is so congenial that I leave with the impression that it was all a matter of courtesy.

December six. Another day I should mark in permanent ink. Shirley and the girls are visiting us when the phone rings:

"Mr. Rodriguez, our company would like to offer you the Junior Accountant position, and I was wondering if we could meet in my office tomorrow at nine." says the Water Board's personnel manager.

"Guess what?" I hang up the phone, trying to catch my breath. "I've been offered a job right on my birthday. Is this being lucky, or what?"

"There's no such thing as luck, Andy. Look at it as a blessing." Coming from the pastor's wife, her words sound profoundly meaningful.

At the tune of $5,000 a year, paid vacation, sick leave, and health insurance—in contrast to bathing a gorilla, faking grief, cleaning maggots, mowing lawns, and servitude—I feel emancipated for the first time in memory. At long last God has granted me employment in that insufferable profession of mine: coat, tie, and dignified.

During training, everyone shows remarkable interest in my development, and little by little, with their phenomenal support, I begin to float on my own.

Allow me to offer my expert opinion that there wasn't in those days another community whose citizens possessed more goodness of heart and generous spirit than those in the Mile High City.

In witness whereof, until hell freezes over; Amen.

CHAPTER 27
A Colorado Christmas

Even though my first paycheck is scheduled to arrive the week of December 17, there won't be enough money left to buy a Christmas tree, much less presents, so we decide that a kiss on the morning of the 25th will suffice. On the other hand how can we let our child's first Christmas pass by without decorations of any kind?

On the night of December 18, around nine-thirty, we hear a loud group of children rattling in front of the house. I have no clue how to scare them off without getting in trouble with something called personal liability, for at work I have been warned about the financial dangers of being accused for saying the wrong thing to the wrong person at the wrong time. Not knowing the legal implications of scolding strange children in terms of losing our savings, the crib, and the fan, I decide it would be best to wait for the crowd to dissipate on its own.

"What would a bunch of kids be doing in our front yard at this time of night? They're going to wake up the baby!" I complain.

Margarita looks out the window. "For heaven's sake, Andy, they're only kids. Stop scaring yourself with that legal stuff someone's put into your head. Who knows? Perhaps all they want is to sell us something, or maybe they have the wrong address."

"Well, at least they should do it quietly, don't you think?"

"Now they're singing songs. Oh, come on, Andy, they can't be that bad. Let's open the door and see what they want. It's Christmas, you know?"

With great concern I unlock the door to a group of Boys and Girl Scouts singing Christmas carols. My fears recede back to below normal.

"Mr. and Mrs. Rodriguez, may we come in?" cries a young boy in the front line. "It's cold, and we're freezing."

"Of course, please make yourselves at home." Margarita shows them in.

Can you imagine thirteen boys and girls trying to find seats inside Mother Goose's living room? What an educational experience!

The last to enter is the lady troop leader. "Every holiday season these kids and their folks prepare a holiday dinner to welcome a family to our neighborhood," she says. "This year you have been chosen."

Margarita offers them hot apple cider they sip to the last drop. Most lie on the floor and others manage to sit here and there. But what amazes me the most are the questions they ask: How big is the Alligator Island? Why did we let Fidel win? Why did we come to Denver instead of Butte, Montana? Would we ever go back? Was the baby Cuban or American? and so on.

The lively bunch stay a little over an hour, and by the time the conversation gets louder and more exciting, the troop leader decides it is late and time to go.

Instead of a personal liability scare, the exchange with eager, curious, kind kids becomes another permanent- marker experience.

Four days before Christmas I come home from work to find our living room stacked with boxes large and small, wrapped in Christmas paper. Bundling up the baby, Margarita is getting ready to go grocery shopping.

"Have you gone crazy? How much did you spend on all this?"

"They're empty, silly. There's nothing inside. I just went to different stores, asked for empty boxes, bought some wrapping paper, and now we're ready for Christmas. And guess what? You, the baby and I are buying a tree tomorrow. It doesn't have to be tall and expensive. Even a nice branch will do."

"Why all this make-believe, when the kid doesn't even know what's going on?"

"Because it's Christmas, Andy; and because it's our first one as a family, can't you understand that?"

As it turns out, we awaken to a thick snowstorm the following morning, coming down in featherlike flakes. We decide to leave the tree idea until we can walk to Lakeside and haul the branch back on foot...even if it is after Christmas. Thus instead of going tree bargaining, we stay home for a Saturday breakfast of pancakes a la Village Inn. Goodness gracious! How I crave those spongy tortillas drenched in maple syrup.

By mid-morning I'm ready to shovel our first significant snow accumulation—over eight inches of wet cottonballs all the way out to the sidewalk, plus the sidewalk. What a drag!

I open the door, shovel in hand, and almost fall flat on my face.

"Margaritaaaa! Come out and take a look at this! Hurry up! For heaven's sake, are you listening?"

"Oh my word, a Christmas tree on our doorstep. How did it get here, ornaments and everything?"

As the baby tries to jump from her arms to touch it, I'm standing on a foot of snow, totally mesmerized.

"It beats the hell out of me. How would I know?"

Through the following months and years we ask the neighbors, the scout master, Bob and Shirley, Carl and Sonya, members of the church, and everyone we know or come in contact with, but amazingly enough no one ever takes credit for such a wonderful deed. It takes us almost forty years to find out that Carl and Sonya had done it...silently, willingly, and lovingly.

And Margarita was correct; a tree without presents and ornaments is nothing but a lifeless bush, right?

Right! So we decide to emulate Scrooge's worst nightmare by throwing stinginess out the window and going to Lakeside on the morning of the 24th to buy real gifts!

One glorious moment after another: All to be stamped in indelible ink on the family's Rosetta stone.

■ ■ ■

A week after Christmas, Shirley took Margarita to see Dr. Haugen, an obstetrician and personal friend of the pastor, because my wife once more was feeling nauseous. The final outcome: she was pregnant...again. The downside this time: the company's health insurance wouldn't cover it. And so in order to generate additional income to pay the rent and cover the unexpected, I began to teach Spanish at night, and during my lunch hour I would copy from the County Clerk's office the names of new homeowners—information I would sell in sticker form to carpet and furniture stores, like Mr. Thompson did in Miami. In order to print the listings I invested ten dollars in an old mimeograph. You can imagine the quality of the print.

For six months, "Jump Publications" sold daily to twelve subscribers for $25.00 a month each. The venture lasted a little over a year, and it made me enough money to pay for the pregnancy and the arrival of the new child.

Our baby girl, Ana Margarita, came to this world during Harvest Moon. Far from Latin-looking, she was born blonde with hazel eyes. Where did she pick up those features? Ask our ancestors.

As nomadic Cubans, the four of us slept in the

same room, with little Ana Margarita in a small crib. *Donde come uno pueden comer cuatro?* Can a plate that feeds one, feed four? The answer is no, unless it is full of baloney.

In those days my father had already sold our De Soto for fifteen dollars, and I had bought a 1953 Pontiac from a friend for one hundred. How could I ever forget that car—the one that blew steam and coolant all over an icy street in the midst of a snow-storm, past midnight, in below-zero temperatures, on New Year's Eve, with the entire family inside.

Shortly after Ana Margarita's arrival, we moved to a bigger home just around the corner. Old and witchy, the seemingly haunted house had two bed-rooms and much more space in which to stretch and move around. Immediately following our move, Carl rented his house to a retired couple for $120.00 month.

With the income from the Spanish lessons and the stickers, I managed to save enough money to buy Margarita a Hensel piano to teach music at home and a St. Bernard puppy, Tom, we would later hire as a stud in exchange for a choice of litter. Since the Holy Spirit apparently didn't work in dogs, however, we only sold one puppy during Tom's five-year life. If all these ventures and part-time jobs weren't enough, Margarita made Cuban piñatas that she sold to a drugstore nearby.

"Do you hit them with a baseball bat?" customers asked.

"These are Cuban piñatas, sir, not Mexican. Just pull the string from underneath and the candy comes out. This way kids won't get hurt," Margarita would answer.

"You should patent these doohickeys before someone else does," the store manager often said.

But the amount of work involved in building these huge contraptions was not worth the bottom line. Besides, Mexicans built them cheaper and the bat was included.

■ ■ ■

Meanwhile, Mima and Don Luis, her hundred-and-six-year-old father, were en route to the U.S. via Mexico- their only way out in those days. Old Don Luis became, if not the oldest, at least one of the oldest immigrants in U.S. history to apply for political asylum.

In the month and year of Colorado's greatest flood, June of 1965, Mima and Don Luis arrived in Denver.

Again, we needed to move into another house. This one was a little bigger and much prettier. The place had many flowers and a huge backyard with enough room for Tom to flirt with his clients.

Two years following the birth of our daughter, once again the Holy Spirit got into the act. I could only marvel at the fact that Hollywood wasn't lying when in the movies women got pregnant with kisses. Boy, was she sensitive...and was I dumb-founded!

Our youngest was also born during Harvest Moon, but in the following year; Richard was the only child who came, as my mother had said, with a loaf of bread under his arm—health insurance, plus countless philosophy degrees. My hat goes off to the family oracle for revolutionizing my way of life during my senior years...without firing a shot.

With our new addition to the family we moved yet again to an even bigger house. Even though the rent was higher, the children's bedroom was still crammed with two boys, a girl, and the St. Bernard, who wouldn't sleep anywhere else but with them. And junk—tons of it, knickknacks that later in life would mutate into antiques, collectibles, and family art. Sentimental stuff that no matter how hard one tries, never disappears.

Quick as a spark plug until the last day, Don Luis died of the Hong Kong flu in that same house at the age of 110, and within a month, our dog Tom got poisoned by one of our friendly neighbors spraying bug-killer on the fence shrubs.

Since it wasn't a lucky house by any measure,

we moved again, this time to the same stronghold in which we have lived ever since. Now a museum in its own right, the house seems priceless when we consider downsizing.

Have you noticed that every old home has a distinctive odor of its own? I believe it's the evocative smell of times gone by, an appeal for gratitude from those it saw loving, crying, laughing, arguing, and praying within the seclusion of its domain.

"I am the witness to your past," our house seems to whisper. "My walls are the custodian of your secrets, the guardian of your treasures—nostalgia I've been hoarding for almost forty years: old toys that don't work, ornaments that crowd each other for attention, dusty books, 8mm movies, slides, photo albums filled with pictures of baptisms, birthdays, Little League baseball, soccer, cheerleading, weddings, first communions...and grandkids. Ah, those grandchildren. The heart and soul of your golden years are mine too; mine to breathe life unto my walls, mine to listen to my stories, mine to tell them who they are and how much I love them."

CHAPTER 28

And They Lived Happily Ever After

Now for the sake of historical accuracy, let's take a detour and rewind the tape back to November 1964.

Longing to keep the family together, my parents, along with Crispin the dog, took a two-thousand-mile leap of affection into the Mile High City. What worried me the most, though, were Papa's dim chances of getting a respectable job at his age and in a town where Spanish still was a foreign language.

Better established, we rented a house for them for a hundred dollars a month and furnished it with the help of friends and the church. Just like us, they fell in love with the surroundings right away. Even my mother's asthma attacks were considerably assuaged by the altitude and the dryness, so they were able to adapt earlier than anticipated.

Just as soon as they touched ground, Papa began to apply for almost every job opening in the classifieds, anything from night watchman and janitor to gas station attendant. Regrettably though, age discrimination was common.

"You're so close to retirement, Mr. Rodriguez," the owner of an employment agency said to him once. "And your English is *so* crude that I honestly think we're both wasting our time."

There were moments when Papa's despondency was so heart-breaking that I prayed for a miracle to happen. It was deeply sad to see an honest man who had worked so very, very hard all his life crash head-on into a granite wall...particularly in the autumn of his life.

On the other hand I also realized that no employer would train anyone for the future when that future had already passed. Did he know a trade? Only an exotic one, the spice trade. Did he have a degree showing some kind of formal education? No, he did not. Did he read and write the language?

Very little. Had he lived in America long enough to know its idiosyncrasies? Not at all. Then what did my father have to offer? Simply the knowledge of his unusual trade and what most older people would: the wisdom and experience that only comes with age. And for that matter, who needed sermons?

But he never gave in. A self-possessed man who looked eagerly into the future, my tireless father wasn't ready to give up, particularly when he felt so confident about the free enterprise system.

Then again, timing also works in mysterious ways, and as their savings dwindled precariously, Dad accidentally found a job on the mixing floor of a small spice company that paid $5.00 hr. The business had four employees, an office manager and three plant workers, and it was owned by an investor who had it as a tax shelter. He didn't know much about the trade and needed someone to help develop new seasoning formulas and to figure out ways to blend and package them for industrial use. With his vast experience in the field, Papa was the perfect candidate for the job.

We had one point of disagreement, though. Papa considered the timely break purely coincidental, and a result of his efforts. I fought him tooth and nail to prove that it was something much more profound than that—a blessing, if not a miracle.

Considering that Denver as our destination was

virtually drawn from a hat, that we didn't know my parents would come after us, that there were no other businesses of its kind within a thousand miles, that the only one needing a person precisely like him existed in the center of town, and that the opening became available when he desperately needed it, why in God's name after these irrefutable proofs did my father still refuse to accept the likelihood of divine intervention? That, if truth be told, I'll never understand.

As it happens with most meaningless tax shelters, the owner eventually lost interest and the business began to suffer. Hence within three years Papa and I were considering buying the company. But in order to do so, first we needed to find the money, and second I had to gather enough guts to quit a secure, well paying job and dive into a venture of unknown depth.

Fate had it that my first chance to own a genuine business would come my way in 1968. Accounting hardly was the love of my life, so after seven years of professional monotony I felt the futility of working in something I didn't like.

In a fusion of Cuban and American values, I sensed that the timing was perfect to shift gears into a more rewarding endeavor, and at twenty-nine I wasn't going to risk that once-in-a-lifetime chance to achieve my next goal: financial independence.

To this end we contacted Mr. Johnson, who was doing very well in his Miami sausage operation at the time, but was cash dry. The man with the brilliant business mind gathered three friends with five thousand dollars each to buy the spice company, conditional on my quitting the Water Board and sticking my neck out with half the income, three kids, a wife, a mother-in-law, and a St. Bernard.

The strategy was for me to develop the business into a profitable venture, while Papa helped from within. It should be said, however, that at the beginning we only owned ten percent of the stock.

In a protracted transaction that lasted well over a year, the company was eventually purchased for $76,000, payable in 144 installments. Like the scroll of a Chinese garden, our path to the American Dream began to unroll before our very eyes.

Thanks to his foresight and sense of fairness, ten years later Mr.Johnson offered Papa and me the entire company at a fair price, and as they say: the rest is history.

Today that venture is a multi-million-dollar industry with Andy, Jr. as president. Some of its employees have been with us from the beginning, and the hardcore team is formed by friends and neighbors who grew up or went to college with our kids.

And now, my devoted reader—tireless, I may add—since I'm about to sail into the sunset, for my story is about to conclude, the time has come to reveal the whereabouts of Margarita and Andy, the two characters who made this memoir possible.

Incredibly enough they're still glued after forty-four years, which is short of miraculous these days. Happily retired, and to keep his nose out of the kitchen during his plenty of free time and also because the capacity of his neurons to release old memories is the only bodily function that improves with age, the heroine's lover has written these pages to ensure that their descendants understand and distill from their recollections, the wisdom and insight embedded in their adventurous past.

What else are they doing with their lives?

For once, they're enjoying their adopted country's natural beauty, taking pleasure in family and friends, and sharing the good things in life, especially the Rocky Mountains and the deep blue sea— the deep blue sea where the most exciting journeys always begin and never end.

Have they become U.S. citizens?

Of course they have.

Have they visited Cuba?

No. Never again until the bastard's gone.

THE END
ADIOS

AKNOWLEDGMENTS

Margarita, for saying *yes, I do*.

Carol Gaskin, from *Editorial Alchemy*
for guiding my pen.

Family and friends for their tremendous support.

The American People, for their generosity.